THINKING LIKE A MOUNTAIN

TOWARDS A COUNCIL OF ALL BEINGS

JOHN SEED JOANNA MACY PAT FLEMING ARNE NAESS

Illustrations by DAILAN PUGH

New
Society
Publishers
Philadelphia, PA

Santa Cruz, CA

Inquiries regarding requests to reprint all or part of
Thinking Like a Mountain should be addressed to:
New Society Publishers
4527 Springfield Avenue
Philadelphia, PA 19143

ISBN: 0-86571-132-1 Hardcover
 0-86571-133-X Paperback
Printed in the United States of America on partially
recycled paper by Wickersham Printing Company,
Lancaster, PA.

Book and cover design by Tina Birky.
Cover and text illustrations by Dailan Pugh.

To order directly from the publishers, add $1.75 for the
first copy, 50¢ each additional. Send check or money order
to:
New Society Publishers
P.O. Box 582
Santa Cruz, CA 95061

A portion of the proceeds from the sale of this book go to
support the work of the Interhelp network and the
Rainforest Information Centre.

New Society Publishers is a project of the New Society
Educational Foundation, a nonprofit, tax-exempt, public
foundation. Opinions expressed in this book do not
necessarily represent positions of the New Society
Educational Foundation.

Acknowledgments

Thanks to the many beings on different continents, who have given form to this work. And to all who have given help, inspiration and encouragement, especially friends in Australia—Interhelp, Lismore; the Rainforest Information Centre; the Big Scrub Environment Centre, Lismore, New South Wales; as well as Trina Shields and Tova Green. In Great Britain, by Gaian providence, Patrick and Stu Anderson have been invaluable. Also appreciative squeaks and grunts to Justin Kenrick, Caroline Wyndham, Bunny Burnell, and the folks at GreenNet in London and their wondrous electronic beings.

"Spirit of Love" by Barbara Deming, excerpted from *We Are All Part of One Another: A Barbara Deming Reader*. Edited by Jane Meyerding, Philadelphia, PA: New Society Publishers, 1984. Reprinted by permission.

"Gatha for All Threatened Beings" by Gary Snyder, excerpted from *Left Out in the Rain*. Berkeley, CA: North Point Press, 1986. Reprinted by permission.

"Beyond Anthropocentrism" was first published in *ECOPHILOSOPHY* 5. Sierra College, CA. It has since been reprinted in *Pantheism, Oikos, Awakening in the Nuclear Age* and several Australian journals.

"Bestiary" by Joanna Macy was first published in "Corona," Montana State University, Bozeman, MT in 1982.

"Gaia Meditation" by Joanna Macy was first published in "Awakening in the Nuclear Age Journal," Issue No. 14, Summer/Fall 1986.

"Oh, Lovely Rock" by Robinson Jeffers was first published in *Such Counsels You Gave Me* (1937), and is reprinted by permission from *Selected Poetry of Robinson Jeffers*. New York, NY: Random House, 1959.

"Passenger Pigeons" by Robinson Jeffers was first published in *The Beginning and the End and Other Poems* and is reprinted by permission from Random House, Inc. New York, NY: Random House, 1963.

About the Title

The North American forester-ecologist Aldo Leopold was one of the first to propose a truly ecological ethic, as far back as the 1930s. His formulation of deep ecology can be found in the exquisite *A Sand County Almanac*. (London, UK: Oxford University Press, 1949). It is the simple maxim, "A thing is right when it tends to preserve the integrity, stability and beauty of the biotic community. It is wrong when it tends otherwise." The chapter "Thinking Like a Mountain" contrasts the interests of the ecosystem with the short-term interests of humans. He demonstrates that unless we can identify with the ecosystem and "think like a mountain," disaster is inevitable.

Spirit of love
That flows against our flesh
Sets it trembling
Moves across it as across grass
Erasing every boundary that we accept
And swings the doors of our lives wide—
This is a prayer I sing:
Save our perishing earth!

Spirit that cracks our single selves—
Eyes fall down eyes,
Hearts escape through the bars of our ribs
To dart into other bodies—
Save this earth!
The earth is perishing.
This is a prayer I sing.

Spirit that hears each one of us,
Hears all that is—
Listens, listens, hears us out—
Inspire us now!
Our own pulse beats in every stranger's throat,
And also there within the flowered ground beneath
      our feet,
And—teach us to listen!—
We can hear it in water, in wood, and even in stone.
We are earth of this earth, and we are bone of its
      bone.
This is a prayer I sing, for we have forgotten this
      and so
The earth is perishing.

Barbara Deming

Contents

Spirit of Love—Barbara Deming i

Invocation: We Ask for the Presence
of the Spirit of Gaia—John Seed 2

Introduction: "To Hear Within Ourselves the
Sound of the Earth Crying"—John Seed 5

Self Realization: An Ecological Approach to
Being in the World—Arne Naess 19

Oh, Lovely Rock—Robinson Jeffers 32

Beyond Anthropocentrism—John Seed 35

Gaia Meditations—John Seed and Joanna Macy 41

Evolutionary Remembering
—John Seed and Pat Fleming 45

Passenger Pigeons—Robinson Jeffers 53

Our Life as Gaia—Joanna Macy 57

Chief Seattle's Message—Chief Seattle 67

Bestiary—Joanna Macy 74

The Council of All Beings
—Pat Fleming and Joanna Macy 79

Testimony of Graham Innes—Graham Innes 91

Gatha for All Threatened Beings—Gary Snyder 96

Guidelines for a Council of All Beings Workshop
—Joanna Macy and Pat Fleming 97

Appendix: Sample Workshop Agendas 114

Suggested Readings 117

About the Authors 119

Publisher's Note—David H. Albert 121

Invocation
John Seed

We ask for the presence of the spirit of Gaia and pray that the breath of life continues to caress this planet home.

May we grow into true understanding—a deep understanding that inspires us to protect the tree on which we bloom, and the water, soil and atmosphere without which we have no existence.

May we turn inwards and stumble upon our true roots in the intertwining biology of this exquisite planet. May nourishment and power pulse through these roots, and fierce determination to continue the billion-year dance.

May love well up and burst forth from our hearts.

May there be a new dispensation of pure and powerful consciousness and the charter to witness and facilitate the healing of the tattered biosphere.

We ask for the presence of the spirit of Gaia to be with us here. To reveal to us all that we need to see, for our own highest good and for the highest good of all.

We call upon the spirit of evolution, the miraculous force that inspires rocks and dust to weave themselves into biology. You have stood by us for millions and billions of years—do not forsake us now. Empower us and awaken in us pure and dazzling creativity. You that can turn scales into feathers, seawater to blood, caterpillars to butterflies, metamorphose *our* species, awaken in us the powers that we need to survive the present crisis and evolve into more aeons of our solar journey.

Awaken in us a sense of who we truly are: tiny ephemeral blossoms on the Tree of Life. Make the purposes and destiny of that tree our own purpose and destiny.

Fill each of us with love for our true Self, which includes all of the creatures and plants and landscapes of the world. Fill us with a powerful urge for the wellbeing and continual unfolding of *this* Self.

May we speak in all human councils on behalf of the animals and plants and landscapes of the Earth.

May we shine with a pure inner passion that will spread rapidly through these leaden times.

May we all awaken to our true and only nature—none other than the nature of Gaia, this living planet Earth.

We call upon the power which sustains the planets in their orbits, that wheels our Milky Way in its 200-million-year spiral, to imbue our personalities and our relationships with harmony, endurance and joy. Fill us with a sense of immense time so that our brief, flickering lives may truly reflect the work of vast ages past and also the millions of years of evolution whose potential lies in our trembling hands.

O stars, lend us your burning passion.

O silence, give weight to our voice.

We ask for the presence of the spirit of Gaia.

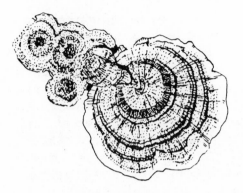

Introduction:
"To Hear Within Ourselves the Sound of the Earth Crying"
John Seed

Our planet is in danger. We all know that on some level of our consciousness. The accelerating ecological crisis which threatens the survival of life on earth is evident now not only to professional biologists, botanists, environmental scientists, but to all of us.

It is evident in the quality of air we breathe, in the food we eat, in the rivers in which we can no longer fish or swim, in the waste dumps leaching their toxins into our water supplies, in news reports about oil spills and acid rain and holes in our protective ozone layer. The tragic disasters of Bhopal, Chernobyl, the Rhine are no longer seen as isolated aberrations, but as part and parcel of a progressive contamination occurring on a steady, mounting, daily basis.

We read staggering statistics: twenty-two acres of rainforest demolished each minute, an area the size of a football field every second of every day. A million species of plants and animals will be extinct by the turn of the century, an average of a hundred a day. Dr. Mustafa Tolba, director-general of the United Nations Environment Program, says that the destruction of genetic material and environments has reached such a pitch that "we face, by the turn of the century, an environmental catastrophe as complete, as irreversible as any nuclear holocaust." These figures and extrapolations of the scientists, combined with the evidences we experience daily are both mind-boggling and numbing. They are so real as to test all our capacities of denial, almost impossible to integrate into the *reality* of the humdrum of our daily lives.

They took on reality for me when I first participated in actions to protect some of the remaining rainforests near my home in New South Wales, Australia. Then I was able to embody, to bring to life, my intellectual knowings in interaction with other beings—protesters, loggers, police, and with the trees and other inhabitants of these forests. There and then I was gripped with an intense, profound realization of the depth of the bonds that connect us to the Earth, how deep are our feelings for these connections. I knew then that I was no longer acting on behalf of myself or my human ideas, but on behalf of the Earth . . . on behalf of my larger self, that I was literally part of the rainforest defending herself.

I knew then, and I know now that these connections—and the knowings and feelings that stem from these connections—are in all of us. I know that we must tap them if we are to stop the destruction and allow the Earth to heal herself. We must find ways to bring forth such realizations in their truth and power in order to arouse and sustain us in defending life on Earth.

I pondered this challenge, seemingly thrown up by the rainforest herself, with Joanna Macy after participating in one of her "Despair and Empowerment" rituals in Australia. We walked and talked in the forests of the

Nightcap Range near my home— the very forests that we had successfully defended some years before. Joanna's work over the years with people from all walks of life had convinced her that it was the destruction of our life-support systems that is the deepest and most pervasive source of anxiety in our time. It is not a hypothetical danger like nuclear war, for it is happening now . . . and people, as much as they would like to deny it, sense it, feel it, often on an inchoate level, in their bodies. The very enormity of the threat makes it harder to talk about it or confront it squarely.

Both of us had been inspired by the writings of Arne Naess, Professor Emeritus of Philosophy at Oslo University, and we understood peoples' widespread though semiconscious awareness of the environmental peril in terms of the deep ecology perspective Naess articulates. We wondered if we could combine "Despair and Empowerment" work and deep ecology in ways that would awaken people's commitment and courage to act for our planet. From our discussions emerged "The Council of All Beings." It is a form of group work which prepares and allows people to "hear within themselves the sounds of the earth crying" a phrase borrowed from Vietnamese Zen master Thich Nhat Hanh, and to let other life forms speak through them. It is a form which permits us to experience consciously both the pain and the power of our interconnectedness with all life.

Soon afterward, the first Council of All Beings took place in a rural setting outside of Sydney, Australia with forty humans participating, to the haunting earthy sounds of the aboriginal *didgeridoo*. Pat Fleming was on hand to assist. Since that early March day in 1985 this form of group work or ritual has been shared by Joanna, Pat, myself, and others with a wide audience in Australia, North America and Europe. The Council of All Beings has been convened in forests, conference centers, schoolrooms and in churches as a central part of the liturgy.

And it was written by people in far-flung places—I'm in Australia, Pat in England and Joanna in Tibet and then California. From letters and phone calls we have received from around the world, each experience has been profound and longlasting.

The Council of All Beings, as we have come to use the phrase both in our work and in this book, refers to both a particular ritual enactment and also to a set of group processes and practices of which the ritual is a part. It is to share this form with a wider public that we make this book available. But first let me explain a bit more about the two streams which flow together here in this new form of group work.

DESPAIR AND EMPOWERMENT

One root of the Council of All Beings is the Despair and Empowerment work developed by Joanna Macy and many others in the Interhelp Network.[1] Many activists who rouse us to the fact that our survival is at stake decry public apathy. They often assume, mistakenly, that people do not change because they lack *information* and that the main job of activists is to provide the missing information. The experience of despairwork suggests that such numbness and apathy does not stem from ignorance or indifference; on the contrary, most of us are aware of the destruction of our planet at the deepest level. But we do not face it, do not integrate it for fear of experiencing the despair that such information provokes. We fear it may overwhelm us. Moreover, our society has constructed taboos against the communication and expression of such anguish.

This refusal of feeling takes a heavy toll on us, impoverishing both our emotional and our sensory lives. It also impedes our capacity to process and respond to information as we screen out or filter anxiety-provoking data. But such feedback is precisely what we need to adapt and survive.

Experience with group work has shown that this despair, grief and anger can be confronted, experienced and creatively channelled. Far from being crushed by it, new energy, creativity and empowerment can be released. Unblocking these feelings also opens us to experiencing our fundamental interconnectedness with all life. Often after such experiences, people come together to form ongoing support groups or join existing groups to take action on peace and/or environmental issues.

DEEP ECOLOGY

> Ecological thinking . . . requires a kind of vision across boundaries. The epidermis of the skin is ecologically like a pond surface or a forest soil, not a shell so much as delicate interpenetration. It reveals the self enobled and extended . . . as part of the landscape and the ecosystem, because the beauty and complexity of nature are continuous with ourselves . . . we must affirm that the world is a being, a part of our own body.[2]

The other root of the Council of All Beings, is a new philosophy of nature called "deep ecology."[3] In contrast to reform environmentalism which attempts only to treat some of the symptoms of the environmental crisis, deep ecology questions the fundamental premises and values of contemporary civilization. Our technological culture has coopted and absorbed all other criticism, so that parts may be questioned but not the whole, while deep ecology as a fountain of revolutionary thought subjects the core of our social existence and our thinking to piercing scrutiny. Deep ecology recognizes that nothing short of a total revolution in consciousness will be of lasting use in preserving the life-support systems of our planet.

Within the framework of deep ecology, and contrary to key assumptions of Judaeo-Christian/Marxist/humanist tradition, humans are not to be viewed as the ultimate measure of value or as the crown of creation. We are but "a plain member" of the biotic community and our arrogance with respect to this community threatens not only ourselves but all of life. We must learn to "let beings be," to allow other species to follow their separate evolutionary destinies without dominating them. We must come to understand that life-forms do not constitute a pyramid with our species at the apex, but rather a circle where everything is connected to everything else. We must realize that the environment is not "out there," and that when we poison the air or the water or the soil, we poison ourselves because of the vast biological cycles within which we too are inextricably embedded. The themes of deep ecology echo the ancient earth wisdom of native peoples such as Chief Seattle (see page 67). They are further elaborated in this volume in "Beyond Anthropocentrism." (See page 35.)

The intellectual acceptance of these concepts is difficult, as our entire socialization in western societies goes against them. An analysis of the political, economic, social and cultural block to a full appreciation of deep ecology would require a book in itself! Furthermore, intellectual acceptance of these concepts is not enough; enormous energies are needed for change to take place on a fundamental level. As Arne Naess points out in his chapter on "*Self* Realization," this knowledge must permeate us and become part of our very identity. This is not to deny our identity as humans but rather, as Naess argues, to place this identity within its proper perspective, within the larger perspective of our "ecological Self." But while full intellectual acceptance of the truths offered by deep ecology might be extremely difficult to attain, through the power of ritual we may be able to capture a glimpse of the possibilities of *Self* which are open to us.

RITUALS FOR TRANSFORMATION

Deep ecology writer and philosopher Dolores LaChapelle in *Earth Wisdom* notes:

. . . rock flour produced by long-ago glaciers has taken about 25,000 years to become fertile soil; yet here in the United States we have lost half of this productive topsoil of our country in about 150 years. Merely throwing these statistics out to be absorbed by the rational brain does little good; but, a ritual setting with chanting and dancing can bring understanding to the older levels of the brain and empathy with the soil itself, as was done in past ages by ritual celebrations.[4]

As within our age and culture our sense of self has shrunk, as anthropocentric religions and science have come to dominate our consciousness, our culture has also lost its understanding of the importance of ritual.

Rituals affirming the interconnectedness of the human and nonhuman worlds exist in every primitive culture. The existence of these rituals attests to the fact that our sense of separation has ancient roots in our species. Their existence also suggests that effort is needed to maintain our union with the rest of nature. They also point to directions where we can search to recover the lost connection. Or, as Dolores LaChapelle puts it, "Ritual . . . facilitates interaction between mind-within-the-skull and mind-outside-the-skull, the environment." We find that though we may be able to discard some of the *beliefs* of the culture into which we emerged, changing the *self* imprinted onto us from the moment of birth requires work. Our *self* was molded by this culture, and tremendous energy is needed to effect substantial transformation.

According to the psychologist Jung, all of the major activities of native peoples were entered into with ceremonies or chants, which:

quite obviously have the psychological aim of canalizing libido into the necessary activity. Complex ceremonies of the Pueblo Indians show how much is needed to divert the libido from its natural river-bed of everyday habit into some unaccustomed activity.[5]

All tribal cultures participate in such practices. As Gary
Snyder says in "The Old Ways":

> The shaman speaks for wild animals, the spirits of plants,
> the spirits of mountains, of watersheds. He or she sings
> for them. They sing through her . . . the whole society
> consults the non-human powers and allows some
> individuals to step totally out of their human roles to put
> on the mask, costume and *mind* of Bison, Bear, Squash,
> Corn or Pleiades; to re-enter the human circle in that form
> and by song, mime and dance, convey a greeting from
> the other realm.[6]

Jung believed that modern mind was quite mistaken in
thinking that it can dispense with such ceremonies and
remember and act effectively upon our interconnectedness
by a mere decision of the will. Without recourse to a
universally shared religious spirit which reaffirms this
interconnectedness and without recourse to a belief in
human centeredness, it is left to ritual and "affective
experiences" to effect this transformation at a profound
level of our being.

In her book *Woman and Nature*, Susan Griffin expresses
the possibilities of this transformation thus:

> I love this bird, when I see the arc of her flight, I fly with
> her, enter her with my mind, leave myself, die for an
> instant, live in the body of this bird whom I cannot live
> without, as part of the body of the bird will enter my
> daughter's body, because I know I am made from this
> earth, as my mother's hands were made from this earth.
> . . . all that I know speaks to me through this earth and
> I long to tell you, you who are earth too, and listen as
> we speak to each other of what we know: the light is in us.[7]

EVOLUTIONARY REMEMBERING

There are many ways of evoking such change in our
identity. Methods for inspiring the experience of deep
ecology range from prayer to poetry, from wilderness vision
quests to direct action in defense of the Earth to the ritual

work described in this book. In the Council of All Beings, we channel the energies released by despair and empowerment and other rituals into facilitating a profound change to deeply ecological awareness. In our experience, "affective education"—learning from the heart and body, and the Council of All Beings is just one example—goes much deeper than the exchange of ideas because it is based on the premise that we already possess within us the knowledge we need, and what is necessary is to bring it to conscious awareness.

The knowledge we require is embedded within us and needs to be awakened. In our mother's womb, our embryonic bodies recapitulate the evolution of cellular life on Earth. We can begin to feel the inner body-sense of amphibian, reptile and lower mammal because these earlier stages of our life are literally part of the ontogenetic development of our neurological system.

Nonhuman memories can surface with particular intensity and authenticity when consciousness is altered by special patterns of breathing. Stanislav and Christina Grof have developed what they call "holotropic" breathing to permit subjects to recapture and resolve significant experiences surrounding their birth. They have found that the material which comes to light goes beyond the biographical and even the human realm to include phylogenetic sequences and episodes of conscious identification with other species and life-forms.

In the "Eco-Breath" workshops conducted in Australia, we have discovered that by employing such breathing rhythms in conjunction with strong *intentions* to transcend our solely human identification, the majority of participants experience remarkable identifications with nonhuman Nature. (See references to "Eco-Breath" work in the "Guidelines to the Council of All Beings Workshop," page 108.)

If we wish to reunite with nature, the first requirement is that we have the *intention* to reestablish this contact. We are descended from thousands of human generations who practiced rituals acknowledging our interconnectedness. Once we set the intention to end the separation we have created, the desired results come naturally from rituals that feel authentic to us. As some are already doing, we can begin to reclaim ancient rituals at the solstices and equinoxes affirming our connections to the changing cycles of the seasons. New rituals—enactments of our intentions—are open to all of us, regardless of our original traditions.

THE COUNCIL OF ALL BEINGS

In the Council of All Beings workshops, we participate in a series of processes that weave together three important themes: mourning, remembering and speaking from the perspective of other life-forms.

Deep ecology remains a concept without power to transform our awareness unless we allow ourselves to feel. The workshops provide a safe place to give voice to what we know is happening to our planet and to acknowledge the pain and begin to come to terms with it, to *mourn* our separation and our loss. Rage may also well up, and a passionate caring. When we stop repressing the pain, a sense of belonging and interconnectedness emerges.

There are many exercises which assist the *remembering* of our rootedness in nature. At each Council, we engage in several sensitizing activities shifting us away from our usual cerebral mode. Guided visualizations (see Gaia Meditation, page 41) make our four-and-one-half billion-year journey present and vivid. Body movements accompanying the evolutionary recapitulation (page 45) tap into our knowledge of previous stages of evolution embedded in our neurological systems.

The Council culminates in shedding our human identity and speaking from the perspective of another life-form. The Council of All Beings narrative (page 79) is an example of the kind of interaction which can then take place. We take time alone to be chosen by a plant, animal or landscape feature that we will then represent at the Council. The structure created for the ritual councils allows for spontaneous expression. Creative suggestions for human action may emerge. Invocation of powers and knowledge of these other life-forms also empowers us.

RITUAL AND ACTION

The relationship between these rituals and the actions we take in defense of nature is complex. In spite of the conceptual dotted lines we superimpose, life is seamless and there is a continuity, flow and exchange between the inner and the outer.

These rituals are not in any way a substitute for other, more direct forms of action. Rather, the rituals prepare us and provide us with a larger context for action. When our strategies are formed and informed by a larger context than our narrow ego selves, when we realize we are acting not just from our own opinions or beliefs, but on behalf of a larger Self—the Earth—with the authority of more than four billion years of our planet's evolution behind us, then we are filled with new determination, courage and perseverance, less limited by self-doubt, narrow self-interest and discouragement. The apathy from which many of us suffer, the sense of paralysis, is a product of our shriveled sense of self. Working with the Council of All Beings, we have found that people experience a deepening identification with the Earth, a renewal of energy to struggle for the protection of wild Nature, and to work for peace.

Ritual also helps us be more aware of the ritualized character of virtually all nonviolent direct action, and thus helps us make these actions more powerful. While at times we may be defending a particular stand of trees or mountain ridge or stream, our defense is also symbolic in that we are making our defense in the name of *all* trees, *all* mountain ridges, *all* streams which need defending, and we are asking all who understand these threats wherever they may be to stand with us. When we are attempting to protect nature against those who would destroy it, we are asking those who would destroy the earth to experience the same transformation which we have undergone, *to remember who they really are*, to step out of their *self-limiting* roles as police, politicians, developers, or consumers and act in defense of their larger *Self*-interest. It is the ritual character of nonviolent direct action which brings us closer to the universal realization, expressed by the feminist-pacifist writer Barbara Deming:

> Spirit that hears each one of us,
> Hears all that is—
> Listens, listens, hears us out—
> Inspire us now!
> Our own pulse beats in every stranger's throat,
> And also there within the flowered ground beneath our
>   feet,
> And—teach us to listen!—
> We can hear it in water, wood, and even in stone.
> We are earth of this earth, and we are bone of its bone.
> This is a prayer I sing, for we have forgotten this and so
> The earth is perishing. [9]

Once we have, to quote the poet Robinson Jeffers, "fallen in love outwards," once we have experienced the fierce joy of life that attends extending our identity into nature, once we realize that the nature within and the nature without are continuous, then we too may share and manifest the exquisite beauty and effortless grace associated with the *natural* world, as the testimony of Graham Innes (page 91) makes all so clear. When we hear the earth speak to us, we are transformed and come to understand our actions from a new perspective. As Dave Foreman, founder of the Earth First! movement, so exquisitely puts it:

Those machines, you know, they're made out of the Earth and therefore they can speak to me and I can hear them because they're made out of the Earth itself. And they hate, I can tell you they hate being used to destroy the Earth. And they say to me "Dave, we really don't want to be doing this—we're tired of being reduced; help us to oxidize."[10]

FOOTNOTES

1. Joanna Macy. *Despair and Personal Power in the Nuclear Age* (Philadelphia, PA: New Society, 1983).
2. Paul Shepard. "Ecology and Man," in P. Shepard & D. McKinley (eds.), *The Subversive Science* (Boston, MA: Houghton Mifflin, 1969).
3. Bill Devall and George Sessions. *Deep Ecology* (Layton, UT: Peregrine Smith Books, Utah 1985).
4. Dolores LaChapelle. *Earth Wisdom* (Silverton, CO: Finn Hill Arts, 1984).
5. C. G. Jung, "On Psychical Energy," in *Contributions to Analytical Psychology* (London, UK: Routledge and Kegan Paul, 1928).
6. Gary Snyder. *The Old Ways* (San Francisco, CA: City Light Books, 1977).
7. Susan Griffin. *Woman and Nature* (New York, NY: Harper and Row, 1979).
8. Gary Snyder. "Wild, Sacred, Good Land" in *Resurgence,* No. 38 (May/June, 1983).
9. Barbara Deming. "Spirit of Love," in Jane Meyerding (ed.), *We Are All Part of One Another: A Barbara Deming Reader* (Philadelphia, PA: New Society, 1984).
10. Jeni Kendell and Ed Buivids. *Earth First* (Sydney, Australia: Australian Broadcasting Corporation, 1987).

Self Realization:
An Ecological Approach
to Being in the World

Arne Naess

{This essay is excerpted from the Fourth Keith Roby Memorial Lecture in Community Science delivered at Murdoch University in Murdoch, Australia, March 12, 1986.}

For at least 2500 years, humankind has struggled with basic questions about who we are, what we are heading for, what kind of reality we are part of. Two thousand five hundred years is a short period in the lifetime of a species, and still less in the lifetime of the Earth, on whose surface we belong as mobile parts.

What I am going to say more or less in my own way, may roughly be condensed into the following six points:

1. We underestimate ourselves. I emphasize *self*. We tend to confuse it with the narrow ego.

2. Human nature is such that with sufficient all-sided maturity we cannot avoid "identifying" ourselves with all living beings, beautiful or ugly, big or small, sentient or not. I will elucidate my concept of identifying later.

3. Traditionally the *maturity of the self* develops through three stages—from ego to social self, and from social self to metaphysical self. In this conception of the process nature—our home, our immediate environment, where we belong as children, and our identification with living human beings—is largely ignored. I therefore tentatively introduce the concept of an *ecological self*. We may be in, of and for nature from our very beginning. Society and human relations are important, but our self is richer in its constitutive relations. These relations are not only relations we have with humans and the human community, but with the larger community of all living beings.

4. The joy and meaning of life is enhanced through increased self-realization, through the fulfillment of each being's potential. Whatever the differences between beings, increased self-realization implies broadening and deepening of the *self*.

5. Because of an inescapable process of identification with others, with growing maturity, the self is widened and deepened. We "see ourself in others". Self-realization is hindered if the self-realization of others, with whom we identify, is hindered. Love of ourself will labor to overcome this obstacle by assisting in the self-realization of others according to the formula "live and let live." Thus, all that can be achieved by altruism—the dutiful, *moral* consideration of others—can be achieved—and much more—through widening and deepening ourself.

Following Immanuel Kant's critique, we then act *beautifully* but neither morally nor immorally.

6. The challenge of today is to save the planet from further devastation which violates both the enlightened self-interest of humans and nonhumans, and decreases the potential of joyful existence for all.

◇   ◇   ◇

The simplest answer to who or what I am is to point to my body, using my finger. But clearly I cannot identify my self or even my ego with my body. For example, compare:

I know Mr. Smith.	*with*	My body knows Mr. Smith.
I like poetry.		My body likes poetry.
The only difference		The only difference
between us is that		between our bodies is that
you are a Presbyterian		your body is Presbyterian
and I am a Baptist.		whereas mine is Baptist.

In the above sentences we cannot substitute "my body" for "I" nor can we substitute "my mind" or "my mind and body" for "I." But this of course does not tell us what the ego or self is.

Several thousand years of philosophical, psychological and social-psychological discourse has not brought us any stable conception of the "I," ego, or the self. In modern psychotherapy these notions play an indispensable role, but the practical goal of therapy does not necessitate philosophical clarification of the terms. For our purposes, it is important to remind ourselves what strange and marvelous phenomena we are dealing with. They are extremely close to each of us. Perhaps the very nearness of these objects of reflection and discourse adds to our difficulties. I shall only offer a single sentence resembling a definition of the ecological self. The ecological self of a person is that with which this person identifies.

This key sentence (rather than definition) about the self, shifts the burden of clarification from the term *self* to that of *identification* or more accurately, the *process of identification*.

What would be a paradigmatic situation of identification? It is a situation in which identification elicits intense empathy. My standard example has to do with a nonhuman being I met forty years ago. I looked through an old-fashioned microscope at the dramatic meeting of two drops of different chemicals. A flea jumped from a lemming strolling along the table and landed in the middle of the acid chemicals. To save it was impossible. It took many minutes for the flea to die. Its movements were dreadfully expressive. What I felt was, naturally, a painful compassion and empathy. But the empathy was *not* basic. What *was* basic was the process of identification, that "I see myself in the flea." If I was alienated from the flea, not seeing intuitively anything resembling myself, the death struggle would have left me indifferent. So there must be identification in order for there to be compassion and, among humans, solidarity.

One of the authors contributing admirably to clarification of the study of self is Erich Fromm:

> The doctrine that love for oneself is identical with *selfishness* and an alternative to love for others has pervaded theology, philosophy, and popular thought; the same doctrine has been rationalized in scientific language in Freud's theory of narcissism. Freud's concept presupposes a fixed amount of libido. In the infant, all of the libido has the child's own person as its objective, the stage of *primary narcissism* as Freud calls it. During the individual's development, the libido is shifted from one's own person toward other objects. If a person is blocked in his *object-relationships* the libido is withdrawn from the objects and returned to his or her own person; this is called *secondary narcissism*. According to Freud, the more love I turn

toward the outside world the less love is left for myself, and vice versa. He thus describes the phenomenon of love as an impoverishment of one's self-love because all libido is turned to an object outside oneself.[1]

Fromm, however, disagrees with Freud's analysis. He concerned himself solely with love of humans, but as "ecosophers" we find the notions of "care, respect, responsibility, knowledge" applicable to living beings in the wide sense.

> Love of others and love of ourselves are not alternatives. On the contrary, an attitude of love toward themselves will be found in all those who are capable of loving others. Love, in principle, is indivisible as far as the connection between *objects* and one's own self is concerned. Genuine love is an expression of productiveness and implies care, respect, responsibility, and knowledge. It is not an *effect* in the sense of being effected by somebody, but an active striving for the growth and happiness of the loved person, rooted in one's own capacity to love.[2]

Fromm is very instructive about unselfishness— diametrically opposite to selfishness, but still based upon alienation and a narrow perception of self. What he says applies also to persons experiencing sacrifice of themselves.

The nature of unselfishness becomes particularly apparent in its effect on others and most frequently, in our culture, in the effect the "unselfish" mother has on her children. She believes that by her unselfishness her children will experience what it means to be loved and in turn to learn what it means to love. The effect of her unselfishness, however, does not at all correspond to her expectations. The children do not show the happiness of persons who are convinced that they are loved; they are anxious, tense, afraid of the mother's disapproval, and anxious to live up to her expectations. Usually, they are affected by their mother's hidden hostility against life, which they sense rather than recognize, and eventually become imbued with it themselves:

> If one has a chance to study the effect of a mother with
> genuine self-love, one can see that there is nothing more
> conducive to giving a child the experience of what love,
> joy, and happiness are than being loved by a mother who
> loves herself.[3]

From the viewpoint of ecophilosophy, the point is this:
We need environmental ethics, but when people feel they
unselfishly give up, even sacrifice, their interest in order
to show love for nature, this is probably in the long run
a treacherous basis for ecology. Through broader
identification, they may come to see their own interest
served by environmental protection, through genuine self-
love, love of a widened and deepened self.

◇   ◇   ◇

As a student and admirer since 1930 of Gandhi's
nonviolent direct action, I am inevitably influenced by
his metaphysics which furnished him tremendously
powerful motivation to keep on going until his death.
His supreme aim, as he saw it, was not only India's *political*
liberation. He led crusades against extreme poverty, caste
suppression, and against terror in the name of religion.
These crusades were necessary, but the liberation of the
individual human being was his highest end. Hearing
Gandhi's description of his ultimate goal may sound
strange to many of us.

> What I want to achieve—what I have been striving and
> pining to achieve these thirty years—is self-realization,
> to see God face to face, to attain *Moksha* (Liberation). I
> live and move and have my being in pursuit of that goal.
> All that I do by way of speaking and writing, and all
> my ventures in the political field, are directed to this
> same end.[4]

This sounds individualistic to the Western mind, a
common misunderstanding. If the self Gandhi is speaking

about were the ego or the "narrow" self *(jiva)* of egocentric
interest, of narrow ego gratifications, why then work for
the poor? For him it is the supreme or universal Self—the
atman—that is to be realized. Paradoxically, it seems, he
tries to reach self-realization through *selfless action*, that is,
through reduction of the dominance of the narrow self or
ego. Through the wider Self every living being is connected
intimately, and from this intimacy follows the capacity of
identification and as its natural consequences, the practice
of nonviolence. No moralizing is necessary, just as we do
not require moralizing to make us breathe. We need to
cultivate our insight, to quote Gandhi again "The
rockbottom foundation of the technique for achieving the
power of nonviolence is belief in the essential oneness of
all life."

Historically we have seen how ecological preservation
is nonviolent at its very core. Gandhi notes:

> I believe in *advaita* (non-duality), I believe in the essential
> unity of man and, for that matter, of all that lives.
> Therefore I believe that if one man gains spirituality, the
> whole world gains with him and, if one man fails, the
> whole world fails to that extent.[5]

Some people might consider Gandhi extreme in his
personal consideration for the self-realization of living
beings other than humans. He traveled with a goat to
satisfy his need for milk. This was part of a nonviolent
witness against certain cruel features in the Hindu way of
milking cows. Furthermore, some European companions
who lived with Gandhi in his ashram were taken aback
that he let snakes, scorpions and spiders move unhindered
into their bedrooms—animals fulfilling their lives. He
even prohibited people from having a stock of medicines
against poisonous bites. He believed in the possibility of
satisfactory coexistence and he proved right. There were
no accidents. Ashram people would naturally look into
their shoes for scorpions before putting them on. Even

when moving over the floor in darkness one could easily avoid trampling on one's fellow beings. Thus, Gandhi recognized a basic, common right to live and blossom, to self-realization applicable to any being having interests or needs. Gandhi made manifest the internal relation between self-realization, nonviolence and what is sometimes called biospherical egalitarianism.

In the environment in which I grew up, I heard that what is important in life is to *be* somebody—usually implying to outdo others, to be victorious in comparison of abilities. This conception of the meaning and goal of life is especially dangerous today in the context of vast international economic competition. The law of supply and demand of separate, isolatable "goods and services" independent of real needs, must not be made to reign over increasing areas of our lives. The ability to cooperate, to work with people, to make them feel good *pays* of course in a fiercely individualist society, and high positions may require it. These virtues are often subordinated to the career, to the basic norms of narrow ego fulfillment, not to a self-realization worth the name. To identify self-realization with ego indicates a vast underestimation of the human self.

According to a usual translation of Pali or Sanskrit, Buddha taught his disciples that the human *mind* should embrace all living things as a mother cares for her son, her only son. For some it is not meaningful or possible for a human *self* to embrace all living things, then the usual translation can remain. We ask only that your *mind* embrace all living beings, and that you maintain an intention to care, feel and act with compassion.

If the Sanskrit word *atman* is translated into English, it is instructive to note that this term has the basic meaning of *self* rather than *mind* or *spirit,* as you see in translations. The superiority of the translation using the word *self* stems from the consideration that *if* your *self* in the wide sense embraces another being, you need no moral exhortation to show care. You care for yourself without feeling any moral pressure to do it—unless you have succumbed to a neurosis of some kind, developed self-destructive tendencies, or hate yourself.

The Australian ecological feminist Patsy Hallen uses a formula close to that of Buddha: "we are here to embrace rather than conquer the world." Notice that the term *world* is used here rather than *living beings*. I suspect that our thinking need not proceed from the notion of living being to that of the world. If we can conceive of reality or the world we live in as alive in a wide, not easily defined sense then there will be no non-living beings to care for!

If "self-realization" today is associated with life-long narrow ego gratification, isn't it inaccurate to use this term for self-realization in the widely different sense of Gandhi, or less religiously loaded, as a term for the widening and deepening of the self so it embraces all life forms? Perhaps it is. But I think the very popularity of the term makes people listen for a moment and feel safe. In that moment the notion of a greater Self can be introduced, contending that if people equate self-realization with narrow ego fulfillment, they seriously *underestimate* themselves. We are much greater, deeper, more generous and capable of dignity and joy than we think! A wealth of non-competitive joys is open to us!

I have another important reason for inviting people to think in terms of deepening and widening their selves, starting with narrow ego gratification as the crudest, but inescapable starting point. It has to do with the notion usually placed as the opposite of egoism, namely the notion of *altruism*. The Latin term *ego* has as its opposite the *alter*. Altruism implies that *ego* sacrifices its interest in favour of the other, the *alter*. The motivation is primarily that of duty; it is said that we *ought* to love others as strongly as we love ourself.

What humankind is capable of loving from mere duty or more generally from moral exhortation is, unfortunately, very limited. From the Renaissance to the Second World War about four hundred cruel wars have been fought by Christian nations, usually for the flimsiest of reasons. It seems to me that in the future more emphasis has to be given to the conditions which naturally widen and deepen our self. With a sufficiently wide and deep sense of self, ego and alter as opposites are eliminated stage by stage as the distinctions are transcended.

Early in life, the social *self* is sufficiently developed so that we do not prefer to eat a big cake alone. We share the cake with our family and friends. We identify with these people sufficiently to see our joy in their joy, and to see our disappointment in theirs. Now is the time to share with all life on our maltreated earth by deepening our identification with all life-forms, with the ecosystems, and with Gaia, this fabulous, old planet of ours.

The philosopher Immanuel Kant introduced a pair of contrasting concepts which deserve extensive use in our effort to live harmoniously in, for and of nature: the concept of *moral* act and that of *beautiful* act. Moral acts are acts motivated by the intention to follow moral laws, at whatever cost, that is, to do our moral duty solely out of respect for that duty. Therefore, the supreme indication of our success in performing a pure, moral act is that we do it completely against our inclination, that we hate to do it, but are compelled by our respect for moral law. Kant was deeply awed by two phenonmena, "the heaven with its stars above me and the moral law within me."

If we do something we should because of a moral law, but do it out of inclination and with pleasure—what then? If we do what is right because of positive inclination, then, according to Kant, we perform a *beautiful* act. My point is that in environmental affairs we should primarily try to influence people toward beautiful acts by finding ways to work on their inclinations rather than their morals. Unhappily, the extensive moralizing within the ecological movement has given the public the false impression that they are primarily asked to sacrifice, to show more responsibility, more concern, and better morals. As I see it we need the immense variety of sources of joy opened through increased sensitivity toward the richness and diversity of life, through the profound cherishing of free natural landscapes. We all can contribute to this individually, and it is also a question of politics, local and global. Part of the joy stems from the consciousness of our intimate relation to something bigger than our own ego, something which has endured for millions of years and is worth continued life for millions of years. The requisite care flows naturally if the self is widened and deepened so that protection of free nature is felt and conceived of as protection of our very selves.

 We need the immense variety of sources of joy opened through increased sensitivity toward the richness and diversity of life, through the profound cherishing of free natural landscapes.

What I am suggesting is the supremacy of ecological ontology and a higher realism over environmental ethics as a means of invigorating the ecology movement in the years to come. If reality is experienced by the ecological Self, our behavior *naturally* and beautifully follows norms of strict environmental ethics. We certainly need to hear about our ethical shortcomings from time to time, but we change more easily through encouragement and a deepened perception of reality and our own *self*, that is, through a deepened realism. How that is to be brought about is too large a question for me to deal with here. But it will clearly be more a question of community therapy than community science: we must find and develop therapies which heal our relations with the widest community, that of all living beings.

FOOTNOTES

1. Erich Fromm, "Selfishness, Self-love, and Self-interest," in *The Self: Explorations in Personal Growth,* edited by Clark E. Moustakas (New York, NY: Harper, 1956), page 58.
2. Ibid., page 59.
3. Gandhi quotations are taken from Arne Naess, *Gandhi and Group Conflict* (Oslo, Norway: Universitetsforlaget, 1974), page 35 where the metaphysics of self-realization are treated more thoroughly in that work.
4. Ibid.
5. Ibid.

Oh, Lovely Rock

We stayed the night in the pathless gorge of Ventana
    Creek, up the east fork.
The rock walls and the mountain ridges hung forest on
    forest above our heads, maple and redwood,
Laurel, oak, madrone, up to the high and slender Santa
    Lucian firs that stare up the cataracts
Of slide-rock to the star-color precipices.

                      We lay on gravel and
    kept a little camp-fire for warmth.
Past midnight only two or three coals glowed red in the
    cooling darkness; I laid a clutch of dead bay-leaves
On the ember ends and felted dry sticks across them and
    lay down again. The revived flame
Lighted my sleeping son's face and his companion's, and
    the vertical face of the great gorge-wall
Across the stream. Light leaves overhead danced in the
    fire's breath, tree-trunks were seen: it was the rock wall
That fascinated my eyes and mind. Nothing strange: light-
    gray diorite with two or three slanting seams in it,
Smooth-polished by the endless attrition of slides and

floods; no fern nor lichen, pure naked rock ... as if I were
Seeing rock for the first time. As if I were seeing through
 the flame-lit surface into the real and bodily
And living rock. Nothing strange . . . I cannot
Tell you how strange: the silent passion, the deep nobility
 and childlike loveliness: this fate going on
Outside our fates. It is here in the mountain like a grave
 smiling child. I shall die, and my boys
Will live and die, our world will go on through its rapid
 agonies of change and discovery; this age will die,
And wolves have howled in the snow around a new
 Bethlehem: this rock will be here, grave, earnest, not
 passive: the energies
That are its atoms will still be bearing the whole mountain
 above: and I, many packed centuries ago,
Felt its intense reality with love and wonder, this lonely
 rock.

—Robinson Jeffers

Beyond Anthropocentrism
John Seed

But the time is not a strong prison either.
A little scraping of the walls of dishonest contractor's
    concrete
Through a shower of chips and sand makes freedom.
Shake the dust from your hair. This mountain sea-coast
    is real
For it reaches out far into the past and future;
It is part of the great and timeless excellence of things. [1]

"Anthropocentrism" or "homocentrism" means human chauvinism. Similar to sexism, but substitute "human race" for "man" and "all other species" for "woman." Human chauvinism, the idea that humans are the crown of creation, the source of all value, the measure of all things, is deeply embedded in our culture and consciousness.

And the fear of you and the dread of you shall be upon every beast of the earth, and upon every fowl of the air, and upon all that moveth on the earth, and upon all the fishes of the sea; into your hands they are delivered. [2]

When humans investigate and see through their layers of anthropocentric self-cherishing, a most profound change in consciousness begins to take place. Alienation subsides. The human is no longer an outsider, apart. Your humanness is then recognized as being merely the most recent stage of your existence, and as you stop identifying exclusively with this chapter, you start to get in touch with yourself as mammal, as vertebrate, as a species only recently emerged from the rainforest. As the fog of amnesia disperses, there is a transformation in your relationship to other species, and in your commitment to them.

What is described here should not be seen as merely intellectual. The intellect is one entry point to the process outlined, and the easiest one to communicate. For some people however, this change of perspective follows from actions on behalf of Mother Earth. "I am protecting the rainforest" develops to "I am part of the rainforest protecting myself. I am that part of the rainforest recently emerged into thinking." What a relief then! The thousands of years of imagined separation are over and we begin to recall our true nature. That is, the change is a spiritual one, thinking like a mountain,[3] sometimes referred to as "deep ecology."

I am that part of the rainforest recently emerged into thinking.

As your memory improves, as the implications of evolution and ecology are internalized and replace the outmoded anthropocentric structures in your mind, there is an identification with all life. Then follows the realization that the distinction between "life" and "lifeless" is a human construct. Every atom in this body existed before organic life emerged 4000 million years ago. Remember our childhood as minerals, as lava, as rocks? Rocks contain the potentiality to weave themselves into such stuff as this. We are the rocks dancing. Why do we look down on them with such a condescending air? It is they that are the immortal part of us.[4]

If we embark upon such an inner voyage, we may find, upon returning to present day consensus reality, that our actions on behalf of the environment are purified and strengthened by the experience.

We have found a level of our being that moth, rust, nuclear holocaust or destruction of the rainforest gene pool do not corrupt. The commitment to save the world is not decreased by the new perspective, although the fear and anxiety which were part of our motivation start to dissipate and are replaced by a certain disinterestedness. We act because life is the only game in town, and actions from a disinterested, less attached consciousness may be more effective. Activists often don't have much time for meditation. The disinterested space we find here may be similar to meditation. Some teachers of meditation are embracing deep ecology[5] and vice versa.[6] Of all the species that have existed, it is estimated that less than one in a hundred exist today. The rest are extinct.

We are the rocks dancing.

As the environment changes, any species that is unable to adapt, to change, to evolve, is extinguished. All evolution takes place in this fashion. In this way an oxygen-starved fish, ancestor of yours and mine, commenced to colonize the land.

The human species is one of millions threatened by imminent extinction through nuclear war and other environmental changes. And while it is true that the "human nature" revealed by 12,000 years of written history does not offer much hope that we can change our warlike, greedy, ignorant ways, the vastly longer fossil history assures us that we *can* change. We *are* the fish, and the myriad other death-defying feats of flexibility which a study of evolution reveals to us. A certain confidence (in spite of our recent "humanity") is warranted. From this point of view, the threat of extinction appears as the invitation to change, to evolve. After a brief respite from the potter's hand, here we are back on the wheel again. The change that is required of us is not some new resistance to radiation, but a change in consciousness. Deep ecology is the search for a viable consciousness. Surely consciousness emerged and evolved according to the same laws as everything else. Molded by environmental pressures, the mind of our ancestors must time and again have been forced to transcend itself.

To survive our current environmental pressures, we must consciously remember our evolutionary and ecological inheritance. We must learn to "think like a mountain."

  Threat of extinction is the potter's hand that molds all forms of life.

If we are to be open to evolving a new consciousness, we must fully face up to our impending extinction (the ultimate environmental pressure). This means acknowledging that part of us which shies away from the truth, hides in intoxication or busyness from the despair of the human, whose 4000-million-year race is run, whose organic life is a mere hair's breadth from finished.[7] A biocentric perspective, the realization that rocks *will* dance, and that roots go deeper than 4000 million years, may give us the courage to face despair and break through to a more viable consciousness, one that is sustainable and in harmony with life again.

> Protecting something as wide as this planet is still an abstraction for many. Yet I see the day in our own lifetime that reverence for the natural systems—the oceans, the rainforests, the soil, the grasslands, and all other living

things—will be so strong that no narrow ideology based upon politics or economics will overcome it.[8]

As Arne Naess, the "father" of deep ecology notes "The essence of deep ecology is to ask deeper questions. . . . We ask which society, which education, which form of religion is beneficial for all life on the planet as a whole."[9]

FOOTNOTES

1. From the poem "A Little Scraping," in the *Selected Poetry of Robinson Jeffers* (New York, NY: Random House, 1959).
2. Genesis 9:2.
3. "The forester ecologist Aldo Leopold underwent a dramatic conversion from the 'stewardship' shallow ecology resource management mentality of man-over-nature to announce that humans should see themselves as 'plain members' of the biotic community. After the conversion, Leopold saw steadily, and with shining clarity as he broke through the anthropocentric illusions of his time and began 'thinking like a mountain.' " George Sessions, "Spinoza, Perennial Philosophy and Deep Ecology" (unpublished, Sierra College, Rocklin, CA, 1979). See Aldo Leopold, *A Sand County Almanac* (London, UK: Oxford University Press, 1949).
4. Prominent physicists such as David Bohm (*Wholeness and the Implicate Order*, London, UK: Routledge, Kegan and Paul, 1980) and biologists and philosophers such as Charles Birch and John B. Cobb Jr. (*The Liberation of Life*, Cambridge, UK: Cambridge University Press, 1981) would agree with Alfred North Whitehead that "a thoroughgoing evolutionary philosophy is inconsistent with materialism. The aboriginal stuff, or material from which a materialistic philosophy starts is incapable of evolution" (*Science and the Modern World*, New York, NY: Macmillan, 1925, page 133). Similar views to those of these authors on the interpenetration of all "matter" (better conceived as "events") are developed in Fritjof Capra's *The Tao of Physics* (Berkeley, CA: Shambhala Publications, 1975) while the sixth century B.C. *Tao Te Ching* itself tells us that "Tao" or "the implicate order" as Bohm might say, "is the source of the ten thousand things" (translator G. Feng and J. English, New York, NY: Vintage, 1972).

When one thinks like a mountain, one thinks also like the black bear, so that honey dribbles down your fur as you catch the bus to work.

5. "For Dogen Zenji, the others who are 'none other than myself' include mountains, rivers, and the great earth. When one thinks like a mountain, one thinks also like the black bear, so that honey dribbles down your fur as you catch the bus to work." Robert Aitken Roshi, Zen Buddhist teacher,

"Gandhi, Dogen and Deep Ecology," in *The Mind of Clover: Essays in Zen Buddhist Ethics* (San Francisco, CA: North Point Press, 1984).

6. Theodore Roszak, for example, has written in *Person/Planet* (Garden City, NY: Anchor Press/Doubleday, 1978) "I sometimes think there could be no deeper criterion to measure our readiness for an economics of permanence than silence." Roszak has argued eloquently in another context that if ecology is to work in the service of transforming consciousness, it will be because its students recognize the truth contained in a single line of poetry by Kathleen Raine, "It is not birds that speak, but men learn silence" (*Where the Wasteland Ends*, London, UK: Faber and Faber, 1974, page 404).

7. For the creative use of despair, see Joanna Macy, *Despair and Personal Power in the Nuclear Age* (Philadelphia, PA: New Society Publishers, 1983). For a long look at our impending extinction, see Jonathan Schell, *The Fate of the Earth* (New York, NY: Alfred Knopf, 1982).

8. Jerry Brown, former Governor of California, in "Not Man Apart," Friends of the Earth newsletter, vol. 9, no. 9, August 1979.

9. Interview with Arne Naess by "The Ten Directions," Zen Center of Los Angeles newsletter, Summer/Fall 1982.

Gaia Meditations
John Seed and Joanna Macy

What are you? What am I? Intersecting cycles of water, earth, air and fire, that's what I am, that's what you are.

WATER—blood, lymph, mucus, sweat, tears, inner oceans tugged by the moon, tides within and tides without. Streaming fluids floating our cells, washing and nourishing through endless riverways of gut and vein and capillary. Moisture pouring in and through and out of you, of me, in the vast poem of the hydrological cycle. You are that. I am that.

EARTH—matter made from rock and soil. It too is pulled by the moon as the magma circulates through the planet heart and roots suck molecules into biology. Earth pours through us, replacing each cell in the body every seven years. Ashes to ashes, dust to dust, we ingest, incorporate and excrete the earth, are made from earth. I am that. You are that.

AIR—the gaseous realm, the atmosphere, the planet's membrane. The inhale and the exhale. Breathing out carbon dioxide to the trees and breathing in their fresh exudations. Oxygen kissing each cell awake, atoms dancing in orderly metabolism, interpenetrating. That dance of the air cycle, breathing the universe in and out again, is what you are, is what I am.

FIRE—Fire, from our sun that fuels all life, drawing up plants and raising the waters to the sky to fall again replenishing. The inner furnace of your metabolism burns with the fire of the Big Bang that first sent matter-energy spinning through space and time. And the same fire as the lightning that flashed into the primordial soup catalyzing the birth of organic life.

You were there, I was there, for each cell of our bodies is descended in an unbroken chain from that event. Through the desire of atom for molecule, of molecule for cell, of cell for organism. In that spawning of forms death was born, born simultaneously with sex, before we divided from the plant realm. So in our sexuality we can feel ancient stirrings that connect us with plant as well as animal life. We come from them in an unbroken chain— through fish learning to walk the land, feeling scales turning to wings, through the migrations in the ages of ice.

We have been but recently in human form. If Earth's whole history were compressed into twenty-four hours beginning at midnight, organic life would begin only at 5 pm . . . mammals emerge at 11:30 . . . and from amongst them at only seconds to midnight, our species.

In our long planetary journey we have taken far more ancient forms than these we now wear. Some of these forms we remember in our mother's womb, wear vestigial tails and gills, grow fins for hands.

Countless times in that journey we died to old forms, let go of old ways, allowing new ones to emerge. But nothing is ever lost. Though forms pass, all returns. Each worn-out cell consumed, recycled . . . through mosses, leeches, birds of prey. . . .

Think to your next death. Will your flesh and bones back into the cycle. Surrender. Love the plump worms you will become. Launder your weary being through the fountain of life.

Beholding you, I behold as well all the different creatures that compose you—the mitochondria in the cells, the intestinal bacteria, the life teeming on the surface of the skin. The great symbiosis that is you. The incredible coordination and cooperation of countless beings. You are that, too, just as your body is part of a much larger symbiosis, living in wider reciprocities. Be conscious of that give-and-take when you move among trees. Breathe your pure carbon dioxide to a leaf and sense it breathing fresh oxygen back to you.

 Countless times in that journey we died to old forms, let go of old ways, allowing new ones to emerge. But nothing is ever lost. Though forms pass, all returns.

Remember again and again the old cycles of partnership. Draw on them in this time of trouble. By your very nature and the journey you have made, there is in you deep knowledge of belonging. Draw on it now in this time of fear. You have earth-bred wisdom of your interexistence with all that is. Take courage and power in it now, that we may help each other awaken in this time of peril.

Evolutionary Remembering
John Seed and Pat Fleming

{Notes for conducting the Evolutionary Remembering can be found on page 105.}

PART ONE:
FROM THE BEGINNING OF THE UNIVERSE

Let us go back, way back before the birth of our planet Earth, back to the mystery of the universe coming into being. We go back 13,500 million years to a time of primordial silence . . . of emptiness . . . before the beginning of time . . . the very ground of all being . . . From this state of immense potential, an unimaginably powerful explosion takes place . . . energy travelling at the speed of light hurtles in all directions, creating direction, creating the universe. It is so hot in these first moments that no matter can exist, only pure energy in the form of light . . . thus time and space are born.

All that is now, every galaxy, star and planet, every particle existing comes into being at this great fiery birthing. Every particle which makes up you and me comes into being at this instant and has been circulating through countless forms ever since, born of this great cauldron of creativity. When we look at a candle flame or a star, we see the light of that fireball. Your metabolism burns with that very same fire now.

After one earth year, the universe has cooled down to some 13 billion degrees centigrade. It now occupies a sphere of perhaps 17 billion miles in diameter . . . This continues to expand and stream outward. . . .

Some 300,000 years pass while space grows to about one billionth of its present volume and cools to a few thousand degrees—about as hot and bright as the visible surface of the sun. The electrons are now cool enough for the electric force to snare, cool enough for matter to take form.

Matter begins to assume its familiar atomic form for the first time. The first atoms are of hydrogen, then helium and then other gases.

These gases exist as huge swirling masses of super-hot cosmic clouds drawn together by the allure of gravity . . . these slowly condense into forms we know as galaxies and our own galaxy; the Milky Way dances among them. Purged of free electrons, the universe becomes highly transparent by its millionth birthday.

Within the Milky Way, our sun was born about 5 billion years ago, near the edge of this galaxy while the cosmic dust and gas spinning around it crystalized into planets. The third planet from the sun, our own earth, came into being about 4½ billion years ago.

The ground then was rock and crystal beneath which burned tremendous fires. Heavier matter like iron sank to the center, the lighter elements floated to the surface forming a granite crust. Continuous volcanic activity brought up a rich supply of minerals, and lifted up chains of mountains.

Then, about 4 billion years ago, when the temperature fell below the boiling point of water, it began to rain. Hot rain slowly dissolved the rocks upon which it fell and the seas became a thin salty soup containing the basic ingredients necessary for life.

Finally, a bolt of lightening fertilized this molecular soup and an adventure into biology began. The first cell was born. You were there. I was there. For every cell in our bodies is descended in an unbroken chain from that event.

Through this cell, our common ancestor, we are related to every plant and animal on the earth.

PART TWO: MEDITATION ON THE EVOLUTION OF ORGANIC LIFE

Remember that cell awakening. *BE* that cell awakening (as indeed you are). We are all composed of that cell which grew, diversified, multiplied and evolved into all the biota of the earth.

What does it feel like to reproduce by dividing into two parts that were me and now *we* go our separate ways?

Now, some hundreds of millions of years have passed. First we were algae, the original green plants, then the first simple animals. The algae started to produce oxygen as a byproduct of photosynthesis and this over a billion years or so created a membrane of ozone, filtering out some of the fiercest solar rays.

Now I am a creature in the water. For 2½ billion years, simple forms of life washed back and forth in the ocean currents. Imagine them as I speak their names: coral, snails, squid, worms, insects, spiders. Imagine yourself as perhaps a simple worm or an early coral living in the warm sea. Feel your existence at this time for it remains within each of your cells, the memories of this period in your childhood.

FISH: This was followed by the evolution of fish and other animals with backbones. How does it feel to have a flexible backbone? . . . How do you move through the water as a fish?

Lying belly down, staying in one place, begin to experience gentle side-to-side rolling, with your head, torso and lower body moving all as one. How does the world look, feel . . . sound?   Be aware of your backbone, your head and gills. What does it feel like to move through the ocean, to listen through the ocean?

AMPHIBIAN: Finally about 450 million years ago the first plants emerged from the water and began to turn the rock into soil, preparing the ground for animals to follow. The first animals to emerge from the seas were the amphibians . . . slowly use your forearms to drag your body along. Pull with your left and right together . . . as amphibians we are still very dependent on the water, especially for our reproductive cycle.

REPTILE: It wasn't until the evolution of the reptilian amniotic egg that we were liberated from our dependence on water and able to move completely onto dry land . . . still crawling on your belly start to use legs coordinated with arms, alternating from one side to the other. Notice how our range of movement and perception changes . . . By 200 million years ago, we had successfully moved onto the land.

EARLY MAMMAL: As mammals we became warm-blooded. Remember how as a reptile you used to have to wait, sluggish, for the sun to warm you? The sun now fuels your metabolism in a more complex way. What are the advantages of this?

Living in holes, alert, sense of smell, sampling molecules from the air. To breed before being consumed. All of us are descended from this pedigree for 4 billion years. At every step billions fell by the wayside but each of us was there. In this game, to throw tails once is to fall by the wayside, extinct, a ghost.

Imagine yourself as a lemur, or perhaps as a small cat . . . Notice how supple your spine feels . . . Now with your belly off the floor, begin crawling on your hands and knees. How does this new-found freedom feel? How does your head move?

Now our young need to be looked after until they can fend for themselves.

EARLY MONKEY: Begin moving on hands and feet with greater lightness, leaping and climbing. Discover more flexibility in movement of the spine, head and neck. Make sounds. Notice increasing playfulness and curiosity. We move through the trees, running along branches and swinging through them, our strong opposable thumbs giving us the grip we need. Our sensitive fingertips (with nails instead of claws) able to judge the ripeness of fruit or groom. Agile balance and keen vision develop. We eat food on the spot where we find it.

GREAT APE: Our body becomes heavier and stronger. We can squat erect but use knuckles to walk. Experiment with balancing. How does the world look and smell? Communication?

Ten million years ago a major climatic change began and the forests, home of the ape, began to retreat to the mountains and were replaced by woodland and open savannah.

EARLY HUMAN: It is here on the open savannah that we first learnt to walk on two legs . . . standing on two feet with strong jaw thrust forward. How does it feel?

Vulnerable but inventive and adaptable. Able to look up and easily see the sky. We postpone eating food until it can be brought back to camp and shared. We live in families, discover language, catch fire, make art, music, tools . . . the complexities and subtleties of cooperating successfully with others in a group involves the development of language, the telling of stories, the use of tools, the making of fires.

About 100,000 years ago during the warm interglacial period, a new hominid species emerged called Neanderthal. They bury their dead, sometimes with flint tools—many in a fetal position suggesting a return to the womb of Mother Earth for rebirth, often in graves lying on an east/west axis—on the path of the sun which is reborn every day—their practice of burying the dead shows a dramatic increase in human self-consciousness. Now physical evolution stands still and cultural evolution takes over.

MODERN HUMAN: Developing farming, working on the land, in market places, moving to town—seeing houses, temples, skyscrapers, walking through busy streets, driving in cars, what do you see and hear and smell and feel? How does it feel to be dwelling more often in cities? How have you become more separate from the earth? Now you are pushing your way through a crowded street, you are in a hurry . . . everyone is in your way.

FUTURE HUMAN: The possible human: to the extent that we can surrender our tiny self to our actual, biological being, we can then manifest the powerful erotic energy of evolution and then our personalities slowly come to partake of the nature of evolution, the nature of this planet home.

Sitting down quietly by yourself . . . in your mind's eye, open to any glimpses, images, forms that are waiting to emerge as future human life . . . potential in us that is waiting to awaken a larger ecological Self, living fully as part of nature expressing our full potential in whatever way may occur to us . . . form.

Now slowly come back and, opening your eyes, find a partner close by and sit with them. Taking turns speaking, going back over the stages you remember, describing in the first person what you experienced, what you noticed about each life form. Use the present tense—"I am a single cell and I notice . . . " You are now recounting your evolutionary journey, recounting how the cosmic journey has been for you so far.

Passenger Pigeons

Slowly the passenger pigeons increased, then suddenly
  their numbers
Became enormous, they would flatten ten miles of forest
When they flew down to roost, and the cloud of their rising
Eclipsed the dawns. They became too many, they are all
  dead,
Not one remains.
                          And the American bison: their hordes
Would hide a prairie from horizon to horizon, great heads
  and storm-cloud shoulders, a torrent of life—
How many are left? For a time, for a few years, their bones
Turned the dark prairies white.
                          You, Death, you watch for these things,
These explosions of life, they are your food,
They make your feasts.
                          But turn your great rolling eyes
  away from humanity,
Those grossly craving black eyes. It is true we increase.
A man from Britain landing in Gaul when Rome had fallen,
He journeyed fourteen days inland through that beautiful
Rich land, the orchards and rivers and the looted villas:
  he reports that he saw

No living man. But now we fill up the gaps,
In spite of wars, famines and pestilences we are quite suddenly
Three billion people: our bones, ours too, would make
Wide prairies white, a beautiful snow of unburied bones:
Bones that have twitched and quivered in the nights of love,
Bones that have shaken with laughter and hung slack in sorrow, coward bones
Worn out with trembling, strong bones broken on the rack, bones broken in battle,
Broad bones gnarled with hard labor, and the little bones of sweet young children, and the white empty skulls,
Little carved ivory wine-jugs that used to contain
Passion and thought and love and insane delirium, where now
Not even worms live.
                    Respect humanity, Death, these shameless black eyes of yours,
It is not necessary to take all at once—besides that, you cannot do it, we are too powerful,
We are men, not pigeons; you may take the old, the useless and helpless, the cancer-bitten and the tender young,
But the human race has still history to make. For look—look now
At our achievements: we have bridled the cloud-leaper lightning, a lion whipped by a man, to carry our messages
And work our will, we have snatched the live thunderbolt
Out of God's hands. Ha? That was little and last year—for now we have taken
The primal powers, creation and annihilation; we make new elements, such as God never saw,
We can explode atoms and annul the fragments, nothing left but pure energy, we shall use it
In peace and war — "Very clever," he answered, in his thin piping voice,

Cruel and a eunuch.
                    Roll those idiot black eyes of yours
On the field-beasts, not on intelligent man
We are not in your order. You watched the dinosaurs
Grow into horror: they had been efts in the ditches and
    presently became enormous, with leaping flanks
And tearing teeth, plated with armor, nothing could stand
    against them, nothing but you,
Death, and they died. You watched the sabre-tooth tigers
Develop those huge fangs, unnecessary as our sciences and
    presently they died. You have their bones
In the oil-pits and layer-rock, you will not have ours. With
    pain and labor we have bought intelligence.
We have minds like the tusks of those forgotten tigers,
    hypertrophied and terrible,
We have counted the stars and half understood them,
    we have watched the farther galaxies fleeing away from
    us, wild herds
Of panic horses—or a trick of distance deceived the
    prism—we outfly falcons and eagles and meteors,
Faster than sound, higher than the nourishing air; we have
    enormous privilege, we do not fear you,
We have invented the jet-plane and the death-bomb and
    the cross of Christ—"Oh," he said, "surely
You'll live forever"—grinning like a skull, covering his
    mouth with his hand—"What could exterminate you?"

—Robinson Jeffers

Our Life as Gaia
Joanna Macy

Come back with me into a story we all share, a story whose rhythm beats in us still. The story belongs to each of us and to all of us, like the beat of this drum, like the heartbeat of our living universe.

There is science now to construct the story of the journey we have made on this earth, the story that connects us with all beings. There is also great yearning and great need to own that story—to break out of our isolation as persons and as a species and recover through that story our larger identity. The challenge to do that now and burst out of the separate prison cells of our contrivings, is perhaps the most wonderful aspect of our being alive today.

Right now on our planet we need to remember that story—to harvest it and taste it. For we are in a hard time, a fearful time. And it is the knowledge of the bigger story that is going to carry us through. It can give us the courage, it can give us the strength, it can give us the

hilarity to dance our people into a world of sanity. Let us remember it together.

With heartbeat of the drum we hear the rhythm that underlies all our days and doings. Throughout our sleeping and rising, through all our working and loving, our heart has been beating steady, steady. That steady sturdy inner sound has accompanied us all the way. And so it can take us back now, back through our lives, back through our childhood, back through our birth. In our mother's womb there was that same sound, that same beat, as we floated there in the fluid right under her heart.

Let that beat take us back farther still. Let's go back, back far beyond our conception in this body, back to the first splitting and spinning of the stars. As scientists measure now, it is fifteen billion years ago we manifested—in what they call the Big Bang.

There we were, careening out through space and time, creating space and time. Slowly, with the speed of light, in vast curls of flame and darkness, we reached for form. We were then great swirls of clouds of gas and dancing particles—can you imagine you remember? And the particles, as they circled in the dance, desired each other and formed atoms. It is the same desire for form that beats now in this drum and in our hearts.

Ten billion years later, one of the more beautiful swirls of that swirling mass split off from its blazing sun—the sun we feel now on our faces—and became the form we know best. And our lifetime as Gaia began.

◇   ◇   ◇

Touch our Earth, touch Gaia.

Touch Gaia again by touching your face, that is Gaia too.

Touch Gaia again by touching your sister or brother. That is Gaia too.

In the immediate planet-time of ours, Gaia is becoming aware of herself, she is finding out who she is. How rich she is in the multitudinous and exquisite forms she takes.

Let us imagine that her life—*our* life as our planet— could be condensed into twenty-four hours, beginning at midnight. Until five o'clock the following afternoon all her adventures are geological. All was volcanic flamings and steaming rains washing over the shifting bones of the continents into shifting seas—only at five o'clock comes organic life.

To the heartbeat of life in you and this drum, you too, right now, can shift a bit—shift free from identifying solely with your latest human form. The fire of those early volcanoes, the strength of those tectonic plates, is in us still. And it may well be, if things continue the way they are going, that we will all return for a spell to non-organic life. We'd be radioactive for quite a while, but we are built to endure.

For now and in these very bodies of ours, we carry traces of Gaia's story as organic life. We were aquatic first, as we remember in our mother's womb, growing vestigial gills and fins. The salt from those early seas flows still in our sweat and tears. And the age of the dinosaurs we carry with us, too, in our reptilian brain, situated so conveniently at the end of our spinal column. Complex organic life was learning to protect itself and it is all right there in our neurological system, in the rush of instinct to flee or fight.

And when did we appear as mammals? In those twenty-four hours of Gaia's life, it was at 11:30 P.M.! And when did we become human? One second to midnight.

Now let us take that second to midnight that is our story as humans and reckon that, in turn, as twenty-four hours. Let's look back through the twenty-four hours that we have been human.

Beginning at midnight and until two o'clock in the afternoon, we live in small groups in Africa. Can you imagine you remember? We feel pretty vulnerable; we haven't the speed of the other creatures, or their claws or fangs or natural armor. But we have our remarkable hands, opposable thumbs to help shape tools and weapons. And we have in our throats and frontal lobes the capacity for speech. Grunts and shouts turn into language as we collaborate in strategies and rituals. Those days and nights on the verge of the forests, as we weave baskets and stories around our fires, represent the biggest hunk of our human experience.

Then in small bands we begin branching out. We move across the face of Gaia; we learn to face the cold and hunt the mammoth and name the trees of the northern forests, the flowers and seasons of the tundra. We know it is Gaia by whom we live and we carve her in awe and fear and gratitude, giving her our breasts and hips. When we settle into agriculture, when we begin domesticating animals and fencing off our croplands and deciding that they could be owned as private property, when we build great cities with granaries and temples and observatories to chart the stars, the time is eleven fifty-eight. Two minutes to midnight.

At eleven fifty-nine comes a time of quickening change: we want to chart the stars within as well as those we see in the skies; we want to seek the authority of inner experience. To free the questing mind we set it apart from Gaia. We make conjectures and rules and heroes to help us chart our freedoms to think and act. The great religions of our planet-time arise. At six seconds to midnight comes a man called Buddha and shortly after another called Jesus of Nazareth.

What now shapes our world—our industrial society with its bombs and bulldozers—has taken place in the last few microseconds of the day we have known as humans.

Yet those few microseconds bring us right to the brink of time. And each of us knows that. Each of us, at some level of our awareness, knows that we are doing ourselves in—that Gaia herself, our self, is in danger. And at some level of your consciousness that is why you are here. Oh yes, you may think you are here to heal yourselves on the personal level and find your power in terms of your individual lives. True enough. But we are also here because we know our planet is in danger and all life on it could go—like that! And we fear that this knowledge might drive us insane if we let it in.

Much of the time it is hard to believe that we have come to this—to such an apocalyptic moment. Even those of us who work hard to stop nuclear weapons have trouble really believing that they exist. After the millions of years of life on earth, after the millenia of our civilizations, after Ishtar and Shakespeare and Gandhi and Dorothy Day, we find it hard to credit the fact that we are deliberately manufacturing and deploying these weapons, targeting them at great populations, poising them on hair-trigger alert, leaving them liable to go off on a computer malfunction . . .

So we are now at a point unlike any other in our story. I suspect that we have, in some way, chosen to be here at this culminating chapter or turning point. We have opted to be alive when the stakes are high, to test everything we have ever learned about interconnectedness, about courage—to test it now when Gaia is ailing and her children are ill. We are alive right now when it could be curtains for conscious life on this beautiful water planet hanging there like a jewel in space. Our foremothers and forefathers faced nothing quite like this, because every generation before us took it for granted that life would continue. Each lived with that tacit assumption. Personal death, wars, plagues were ever encompassed in that larger assurance that life would continue. That assurance is lost now and we are alive at the time of that great loss. It is not the loss of the future. It is the loss of the certainty that there will be a future. It affects everyone, whether they work in the Pentagon or the peace movement. And the toll it takes has barely begun to be measured.

In so-called primitive societies rites of passage are held for adolescents, because it is in adolescence that the fact of personal death or mortality is integrated into the personality. The individual goes through the prescribed ordeal of the initiation rite in order to integrate that knowledge, so that he or she can assume the rights and responsibilities of adulthood. That is what we are doing right now on the collective level, in this planet-time. We are confronting and integrating into our awareness our collective mortality as a species. We must do that so that we can wake up and assume the rights and responsibilities of planetary adulthood—so that we can grow up! That is, in a sense, what we are doing here.

When you go out from here, please keep listening to the drumbeat. You will hear it in your heart. And as you hear it, remember that it is the heartbeat of the universe as well, and of Gaia your planet and your larger Self.

When you return to your communities to organize, saying no to the machinery of death and yes to life, remember your true identity. Remember your story, our story. Clothe yourself in your true authority. You speak not only as yourself or for yourself. You were not born yesterday. You have been through many dyings and know in your heartbeat and bones the precarious, exquisite balance of life. Out of that knowledge you can speak and act. You will speak and act with the courage and endurance that has been yours through the long, beautiful aeons of your life story as Gaia.

Chief Seattle's Message
Chief Seattle

{Chief Sealth, or Seattle as he is now known, delivered a speech in his native Duwamish to his tribal assembly in the Pacific Northwest in 1854. Notes on the speech were jotted down by one Dr. Henry Smith, who emphasized that his own English, which reflects the usage of his time—including the use of the generic male which may or may not have been found in the original—was inadequate to render the beauty of Sealth's imagery and thought.

The version we now have was in fact recreated from Dr. Smith's jottings by film scriptwriter Ted Perry in 1970. We should note that it contains several historical distortions and anachronisms: Sealth, a Northwest Indian, would never have seen a prairie and unlikely a buffalo, and no railway was built anywhere near his territory until 1869. We recommend his "testimony," not as a historical document, but for its usefulness in eliciting a response from the listener/reader.}

The Great Chief in Washington sends word that he wishes to buy our land.

The Great Chief also sends us words of friendship and good will. This is kind of him, since we know he has little need of our friendship in return.

But we will consider your offer. For we know that if we do not sell, the white man may come with guns and take our land.

How can you buy or sell the sky, the warmth of the land? This idea is strange to us.

If we do not own the freshness of the air and the sparkle of the water, how can you buy them?

Every part of this earth is sacred to my people. Every shining pine needle, every sandy shore, every mist in the dark woods, every clearing, and humming insect is holy in the memory and experience of my people. The sap which courses through the trees carries the memories of the red man.

The white man's dead forget the country of their birth when they go to walk among the stars. Our dead never forget this beautiful earth, for it is the mother of the red man. We are part of the earth and it is part of us.

The perfumed flowers
are our sisters;
the deer, the horse, the great eagle,
these are our brothers.
The rocky crests,
the juices of the meadows,
the body heat of the pony, and man—
all belong to the same family.

So, when the Great Chief in Washington sends word that he wishes to buy our land, he asks much of us.

The Great Chief sends word he will reserve us a place so that we can live comfortably to ourselves. He will be our father and we will be his children.

So we will consider your offer to buy our land. But it will not be easy. For this land is sacred to us.

The shining water that moves in the streams and rivers is not just water but the blood of our ancestors. If we sell you our land, you must remember that it is sacred, and you must teach your children that it is sacred and that each ghostly reflection in the clear water of the lakes tells of events and memories in the life of my people. The water's murmur is the voice of my father's father.

The rivers are our brothers, they quench our thirst. The rivers carry our canoes, and feed our children. If we sell you our land, you must remember, and teach your children, that the rivers are our brothers—and yours, and you must henceforth give the rivers the kindness you would give any brother.

The red man has always retreated before the advancing white man, as the mist of the mountains runs before the morning sun. But the ashes of our fathers are sacred. Their graves are holy ground, and so these hills, these trees, this portion of the earth is consecrated to us. We know that the white man does not understand our ways. One portion of land is the same to him as the next, for he is a stranger who comes in the night and takes from the land whatever he needs. The earth is not his brother, but his enemy, and when he has conquered it, he moves on. He leaves his fathers' graves behind, and he does not care. He kidnaps the earth from his children, he does not care. His fathers' graves and his children's birthright are forgotten. He treats his mother, the earth, and his brother, the sky, as things to be bought, plundered, sold like sheep or bright beads. His appetite will devour the earth and leave behind only a desert.

I do not know. Our ways are different from your ways. The sight of your cities pains the eyes of the red man. But perhaps it is because the red man is a savage and does not understand.

There is no quiet place in the white man's cities. No place to hear the unfurling of leaves in the spring or the rustle of insect's wings. But perhaps it is because I am a savage and do not understand. The clatter only seems to insult the ears. And what is there to life if a man cannot hear the lonely cry of the whippoorwill or the arguments of the frogs around a pond at night? I am a red man and do not understand. The Indian prefers the soft sound of the wind darting over the face of a pond, and the smell of the wind itself, cleansed by a midday rain or scented with the piñon pine.

The air is precious to the red man, for all things share the same breath—the beast, the tree, the man, they all share the same breath. The white man does not seem to notice the air he breathes. Like a man dying for many days, he is numb to the stench. But if we sell you our land, you must remember that the air is precious to us, that the air shares its spirit with all the life it supports. The wind that gave our grandfather his first breath also receives his last sigh. And the wind must also give our children the spirit of life. And if we sell you our land, you must keep it apart and sacred, as a place where even the white man can go to taste the wind that is sweetened by the meadow's flowers.

So we will consider your offer to buy the land. If we decide to accept, I will make one condition: The white man must treat the beasts of this land as his brothers.

I am a savage and I do not understand any other way. I have seen a thousand rotting buffalos on the prairie, left by the white man who shot them from a passing train. I am a savage and I do not understand how the smoking iron horse can be more important than the buffalo that we kill only to stay alive.

What is man without the beasts? If all the beasts were gone, men would die from a great loneliness of spirit. For whatever happens to the beasts soon happens to the man. All things are connected.

You must teach your children that the ground beneath their feet is the ashes of our grandfathers. So that they will respect the land, tell your children that the earth is rich with the lives of our kin. Teach your children what we have taught our children, that the earth is our mother. Whatever befalls the earth befalls the sons of the earth. If men spit upon the ground, they spit upon themselves.

This we know. The earth does not belong to man; man belongs to the earth. This we know. All things are connected like the blood which unites one family. All things are connected.

Whatever befalls the earth befalls the sons of the earth. Man does not weave the web of life, he is merely a strand in it. Whatever he does to the web, he does to himself.

But we will consider your offer to go to the reservation you have for my people. We will live apart, and in peace. It matters little where we spend the rest of our days. Our children have seen their fathers humbled in defeat. Our warriors have felt shame, and after defeat they turn their days in idleness and contaminate their bodies with sweet foods and strong drink. It matters little where we spend the rest of our days. They are not many. A few more hours, a few more winters, and none of the children of the great tribes that once lived on this earth or that roam now in small bands in the woods will be left to mourn the graves of a people once as powerful and hopeful as yours. But why should I mourn the passing of my people? Tribes are made of men, nothing more. Men come and go, like the waves of the sea.

Even the white man, whose God walks and talks with him as friend to friend, cannot be exempt from the common destiny. We may be brothers after all; we shall see. One thing we know, which the white man may one day discover—our God is the same God. You may think now that you own Him as you wish to own our land, but you cannot. He is the God of man and His compassion is equal for the red man and the white. This earth is precious to Him and to harm the earth is to heap contempt on its Creator. The whites too shall pass—perhaps sooner than all other tribes.

But in your perishing you will shine brightly, fired by the strength of the God who brought you to this land and for some special purpose gave you dominion over this land and over the red man. That destiny is a mystery for us, for we do not understand when the buffalo are slaughtered, the wild horses are tamed, the secret corners of the forest heavy with the scent of many men and the view of the ripe hills blotted by talking wires.

Where is the thicket? Gone. Where is the eagle? Gone. And what is it to say goodbye to the swift pony and the hunt? The end of living and the beginning of survival.

So we will consider your offer to buy our land. If we agree it will be to secure the reservation you have promised. There, perhaps, we may live out our brief days as we wish. When the last red man has vanished from this earth, and his memory is only the shadow of a cloud moving across the prairie, those shores and forests will still hold the spirits of my people. For they love this earth as the new-born loves its mothers' heartbeat. So if we sell you our land, love it as we've loved it. Care for it as we've cared for it. Hold in your mind the memory of the land as it is when you take it. And with all your strength, with all your mind, with all your heart, preserve it for your children and love it . . . as God loves us all.

One thing we know. Our God is the same God. This earth is precious to Him. Even the white man cannot be exempt from the common destiny. We may be brothers after all. We shall see.

Bestiary

Joanna Macy

The earth obey'd and straight
Opening her fertile womb teem'd at a birth
Innumerous living creatures, perfect forms,
Limb'd and full-grown . . .
John Milton, *Paradise Lost,* VII, 453

short-tailed albatross
   whooping crane
      gray wolf
         peregrine falcon
            hawksbill turtle
               jaguar
                  rhinoceros

In Geneva, the international tally of endangered species, kept up to date in looseleaf volumes, is becoming too heavy to lift. Where do we now record the passing of life? What funerals or farewells are appropriate?

reed warbler
   swallow-tail butterfly

Manx shearwater
Indian python
howler monkey
sperm whale
blue whale

Dive me deep, brother whale, in this time we have left. Deep in our mother ocean where once I swam, gilled and finned. The salt from those early seas still runs in my tears. Tears are too meager now. Give me a song . . . a song for a sadness too vast for my heart, for a rage too wild for my throat.

anteater
antelope
grizzly bear
brown bear
Bactrian camel
Nile crocodile
American alligator

Ooze me, alligator, in the mud whence I came. Belly me slow in the rich primordial soup, cradle of our molecules. Let me wallow again, before we drain your swamp, before we pave it over and blast it to ash.

gray bat
ocelot
marsh mouse
blue pike
red kangaroo
Aleutian goose
Audouin's seagull

Quick, lift off. Sweep me high over the coast and out, farther out. Don't land here. Oil spills coat the beach, rocks, sea. I cannot spread my wings glued with tar. Fly me from what we have done, fly me far.

golden parakeet
   African ostrich
      Florida panther
         Galapagos penguin
            Imperial pheasant
               leopard
                  Utah prairie dog

Hide me in a hedgerow, badger. Can't you find one? Dig me a tunnel through leaf mold and roots, under the trees that once defined our fields. My heart is bulldozed and plowed over. Burrow me a labyrinth deeper than longing.

thick-billed parrot
   zone-tailed pigeon
      desert bandicoot
         Southern bald eagle
            California condor
               lotus blue butterfly

Crawl me out of here, caterpillar. Spin me a cocoon. Wind me to sleep in a shroud of silk, where in patience my bones will dissolve. I'll wait as long as all creation if only it will come again—and I take wing.

Atlantic Ridley turtle
   pearly mussel
      helmeted hornbill
         sea otter
           humpback whale
             monk seal
               harp seal

Swim me out beyond the ice floes, mama. Where are you? Boots squeeze my ribs, clubs drum my fur, the white world goes black with the taste of my blood.

gorilla
   gibbon
      sand gazelle

> swamp deer
> musk deer
> cheetah
> chinchilla
> Asian elephant
> African elephant

Sway me slowly through the jungle. There still must be jungle somewhere, my heart drips with green secrets. Hose me down by the waterhole, there is buckshot in my hide. Tell me old stories while you can remember.

> fan-tailed flycatcher
> flapshell tortoise
> crested ibis
> hook-billed kite
> bobcat
> frigate bird

In the time when his world, like ours, was ending, Noah had a list of the animals, too. We picture him standing by the gangplank, calling their names, checking them off on his scroll. Now we also are checking them off.

> ivory-billed woodpecker
> brown pelican
> Florida manatee
> Canada goose

We reenact Noah's ancient drama, but in reverse, like a film running backwards, the animals exiting.

> ferret
> curlew
> cougar
> wolf

Your tracks are growing fainter. Wait. Wait. This is a hard time. Don't leave us alone in a world we have wrecked.

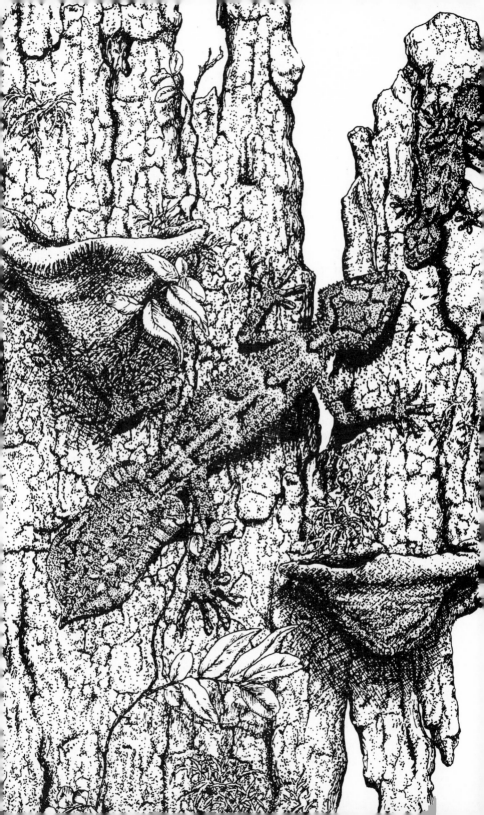

The Council of All Beings
Pat Fleming and Joanna Macy

{This narrative recreates a Council of All Beings ritual conducted out-of-doors in a wilderness setting. The ritual has also taken place indoors and in urban areas. The "Guidelines for a Council of All Beings Workshop" (page 97) offers advice on preparing and leading a Council in either indoor or outdoor environments.}

Some twenty-five of us are gathered at a riverside wilderness site in New South Wales, Australia. Last night we shared stories from our experiences which awakened our concern—even anguish—over what is happening to the natural world in our time. Although we come from different backgrounds, we have this concern in common and it has brought us here to work together. We want to strengthen our courage and commitment to take action to heal our world.

We took time to honor that intention as we first sat down together last night. It has called us to experiment with new ways of healing our separation from nature which is at the root of the destruction of the forests, the poisoning of the seas and soil. These ways of reconnecting are not so new, after all, as Sheila, one of the weekend's co-leaders, pointed out.

> As we explore different group processes for reconnecting with nature, we discover that it is not hard to find ones which work and feel authentic to us. This is not surprising when we consider the thousands of generations of humans who have participated in such processes, and how few the generations since we temporarily forgot them.

This morning we engaged in a number of group exercises to help make us more conscious of our embeddedness in the web of life. They helped us *remember* our bio-ecological history, as our species and its forebears evolved through four and a half billion years of this planet's life. They helped us relax into our bodies, into our intuitive knowings, and our trust in each other. Now, after clearing up after lunch, we assemble to prepare ourselves for the promised ritual of the Council of All Beings.

Instead of beginning right away, we receive from our co-leader Frank an invitation to disperse and go off alone for an hour.

> Find a place that feels special to you and simply be there, still and waiting. Let another life-form occur to you, one for whom you will speak at this afternoon's Council of All Beings. No need to try to make it happen. Just relax and let yourself be chosen by the life-form that wishes to speak through you. It could be a form of plant or animal life, or an ecological feature like a piece of land or a body of water. Often the first that occurs to you is what is right for you at this gathering.

Even before I sit down quietly on the warm sand beside the river I have a sense of the "being" that awaits to emerge in me. It is Mountain.

I relax and breathe in, breathe in Mountain . . . I feel my rock-roots go deep deep down to where the Earth herself is very hot. My base is wide, very wide and solid. Storms come and go over my surface, leaving but a ruffle in my tree-skin. Even the occasional quake of Earth only causes me to shiver and sense more keenly my vitality. I am ancient. I am aware of the centuries, the millenia passing, many seasons and cycles of change. I feel very strong, able to withstand a great deal. Out of this strength I offer protection and shelter to many other life-forms. I also offer inspiration and challenge: the call to come and know me better, to explore my rocks, valleys, and tree-lined rivers. I feel great peace within—immovable, beyond time. I offer this to all who rest upon me. Yet humans, like ants upon my flanks, can be so intrusive, abusive. They gouge my bones, strip flesh, bring danger to my inhabitants. I must speak of this at the Council this afternoon.

Brmm, brmm . . . the drum calls us back. It summons us all back to take time to make our masks and to explore further together our various life-forms. In companionable silence our hands reach for paper, colors, paste-pot. Under the rustling trees are sounds of cutting, folding, breathing.

Brmm, brmm . . . the drum calls us once again, this time to enter the ritual ground and convene as the Council of All Beings. Wearing my Mountain mask of earth, stone, leaves and grasses, I move heavily and slowly toward the ritual ground. The water of the stream that borders the site is cool, washing away the old, preparing us for the new, the unknown. As we gather in a large circle I look around at all the assembled Beings—such an array of forms and colors, some brash, some shy and subtle. An air of uncertainty, yet expectation hangs between us. The gum trees and old fella-grass tree bounding the site rustle in anticipation. A white egret flies past us upstream, flapping its well wishes to our gathering. I settle into the sand, solid, strong, waiting—ready for eternity if need be.

Frank briefs us first on the structure of the ritual. I recognize a blending of different native traditions of our planet's peoples. Through fire and water, we will ritually cleanse ourselves and the ritual ground. To acknowledge the full breadth of our concerns, we will invoke and invite into our circle the earth powers and beings that surround our lives in this space and time: the powers of the four directions and the beings of the three times. Then as the Council proper begins, we will, as the life-forms we have assumed, speak spontaneously, letting be said what needs to be said.

These utterances, we are told, will fall into three stages. From the perspective of the other life-forms we will speak spontaneously among ourselves. We will say why we have come to the Council and be free to express our confusion, our grief and anger and fear. Then, after a while, to the signal of a drumbeat, five or six of us at a time will move to sit in the center of the circle to listen in silence as humans. We'll each have the opportunity to shift between human and nonhuman roles. And lastly we will have the chance to offer to the humans (and receive as humans) the powers that are needed to stop the destruction of our world. Frank offers this overview of the structure to help us feel at ease with the structure of the ritual. He adds that fortunately we do not need to hold its sequence in our minds, for we will respond naturally as the ritual unfolds.

Now with the slow beat of drum and the lighting of fragrant leaves, the Council ritual begins. An abalone shell with burning sage and cedar passes from hand to hand; we inhale the sweet pungent smoke, waving it over our faces. We acknowledge our kinship with fire. Next a glass bowl of fresh water comes round the circle. Each dips into it to anoint the head of the next person, acknowledging our need for cleansing and refreshment.

As the four directions are invoked, we turn to the East, to the South, to the West and North. Drawing on the ancient lore of the Medicine Wheel, we all face in each direction, arms upraised, as one of our number evokes in turn and aloud the meanings it can hold. "We invoke and invite the power of the East . . . the power of the rising sun, of new beginnings, the far-sightedness of eagle . . . "

As Mountain I feel special kinship with the North, "powers of stillness and introspection, of waiting and endurance. . . . "

After each invocation, we all join in with a simple, deep, two-tone refrain: "Gather with us now in this hour; join with us now in this place."

Frank, as the ritual leader, now helps us invite the Beings of the Three Times.

> We invite into our circle all those who have gone before. All you who have lived upon Earth and loved and nurtured it, we remember you and call on your wisdom and your hopes. You, our ancestors and teachers, we ask you to be with us in this time. We seek strength and counsel for the saving of the Earth you loved. We say your names.

Spontaneously and all intermingled from around the circle comes the murmur of randomly spoken names—names of Jesus and the Buddha, of Martin Luther King and grandparents, school teachers and spiritual guides.

> We invoke also the beings of the present time. We invite into this circle our families and friends, our neighbors and co-workers and those who have made it possible for us to be here at this camp. You share our hope and fears, and we are here for you, too.

And from the circle rises again a murmur of names . . . "Peter, Adele, Susan, Bob Hawke, Mikhail Gorbachev . . ."

> Lastly we invoke you beings of the future time, you who are waiting to be born. We cannot say your names, for you have none yet that we can know. Yet it is for you that we work to preserve this beautiful planet. And it is from you, too, that we need help to do what must be done.

After a moment of silence, a silence for the generations we hope will come after us, we chant again the refrain that has followed each invocation.

"Gather with us now in this hour; join with us now in this place."

Now we are ready to speak as a Council. We sit and take our masks. We ease out of our solely human identification; we settle into the life-forms that have come to us and that seek expression.

We hold a roll-call of the assembled beings. One by one around the circle, speaking through our masks, we identify ourselves: "I am wolf and I speak for the wolf people." "I am wild goose and I speak for all migratory birds." "I am wheat and I speak for all cultivated grains."

"We meet," Frank says, having donned his mask of prickly stalks and leaves,

> because our planet is in trouble. We meet to say what is happening to ourselves and our world. I come to this Council as weeds. Weeds, a name humans give to plants they do not use. I am vigorous, strong. I love to thrust and push and seed—even through concrete. Pushing through paving I bring moisture and life. I heal the burned and wounded earth. Yet I am doused with poison now and crushed, as are creatures who live in and through me.

In acknowledgment we all reply, "We hear you, Weeds."

> I am woompoo pigeon. Coooo. I live in one of the last pockets of rainforest. I call my song softly through the giant trees and the cool green light. Yet I no longer get a reply. Where are my kind? Where have they gone? I hear only the echo of my own call. I am frightened; that's why I'm here.

"We hear you woompoo pigeon."

> I am black and white cow, fenced in a paddock, far from grass, standing in my own shit. My calves are taken from me, and instead cold metal machines are clamped to my teats. I call and call, but my young never return. Where do they go? What happens to them?

"We hear you, cow."

> The shells of my eggs are so thin and brittle now, they break before my young are ready to hatch. I fear there is poison in my very bones.

"We hear you, wild goose."

One by one they speak and are heard. Rainforest.
Wombat. Dead leaf. Condor. Mud. Wild flower.
A soft voice says,

> They call me slug—that doesn't bother me. I just slip
> along real slow and gentle, nubbling the leaves as I go.
> But, d'you know, just for this, I get mangled and chopped
> up, squashed without even a "how's your uncle?" What
> have I done to deserve this?

Laughter and sympathy; "We hear you, slug."
Red kangaroo, lichen, wild pig, bottle-nosed dolphin.
"We hear you, we hear you."
I know that it is my time to speak out.

> I am Mountain. I am ancient and strong and solid, built
> to endure. But now I am being dynamited and mined,
> my forest skin is being torn off me, my top-soil washed
> away, my streams and rivers choked. I've a great deal to
> address to the humans today.

"We hear you, Mountain."
The drum beats again, announcing the next stage of the
Council. It summons humans to enter the circle to listen.
Five or six of the beings put aside their masks and move
to the center. Sitting back to back facing outward, they
attend silently as the Council continues. When the drum
beats again after several more beings have spoken, they
return to the periphery to be replaced by others; and the
process continues until each of us will have had the chance
to listen as a human.
"Hear us, humans," says Weeds.

> This is our world, too. And we've been here a lot longer
> than you. For millions of years we've been raising our
> young, rich in our ways and wisdom. Yet now our days
> are numbered because of what you are doing. Be still for
> once, and listen to us.

> I am Rainforest. Counted in your human years I am
> over a hundred thirty million years old. If I were one of
> your buildings, you would take precious care of me. But
> instead you destroy me. For newsprint and cheap

hamburgers you lay me waste. You destroy me so carelessly, tearing down so many of my trees for a few planks, leaving the rest to rot or burn. You push needless roads through me, followed by empty-hearted real-estate grabbers who purport to own me. You cause my thick layer of precious topsoil to wash away, destroying the coral reefs that fringe me. I can't stand your screaming machines which tear through my trunks, rip my flesh, reducing hundreds of years of slow growth to sawdust and furniture. How dare you!

Standing up, majestic in his anger, Rainforest continues.

Your greed and folly shortens your own life as a species. When you leave me wasted and smoldering, you foretell your own death. Don't you know that it is from me that you have come? Without my green world your spirit will shrivel, without the oxygen my plant life exhales, you'll have nothing to breathe. You need me as much as your own lungs. I *am* your lungs."

Oh, humans, as Clean Water I was a bearer of life and nourishment. Look at what I bear now that you've poured your wastes and poisons into me. I am ashamed and want to stop flowing, for I have become a carrier of sickness and death.

Possum holds up her hand.

See my hand, humans? It resembles yours. From its print on the soft soil you can tell where I have passed. What mark on this earth will you leave behind you?

Brmm, brmm . . . the drum sounds into the circle. The humans in the center, looking relieved to be leaving, return to the wider circle and resume the masks of their other life-form. A half-dozen others move to the middle as humans and sit close together, some holding each others' hands as they listen.

I am Bottle-nosed Dolphin. I love to roll and leap and play. Yes, humans, to play with you, too, when I can trust you, for we feel great affinity with you. But in the gill-nets you use we tangle and drown. Taking cruel advantage of our friendliness, you use us for military experiments, fix monitors and transmitters on our backs.

You wall us into your sea parks for show. You deny us the chance to swim free and with our kind. I speak for all captive beings! Find your own freedom in honoring ours.

I feel myself beginning to boil inside and know again I must speak.

Humans! I, Mountain, am speaking. You cannot ignore me! I have been with you since your very beginnings and long before. For millenia your ancestors venerated my holy places, found wisdom in my heights. I gave you shelter and far vision. Now, in return, you ravage me. You dig and gouge for the jewel in the stone, for the ore in my veins. Stripping my forests, you take away my capacity to hold water and to release it slowly. See the silted rivers? See the floods? Can't you see? In destroying me you destroy yourselves. For Gaia's sake, wake up!

Humans, I am Lichen. Slowly over the ages I turn rock into soil. I thought nothing could ever stop me. Till now. Now I sicken with your acid rain.

Look on me, humans. I am the last wild Condor of that part of the Earth you call California. I was captured a few days ago—"for your own good," you tell me. Look long and hard at me, at the stretch of my wings, at the glisten of my feathers, the gleaming of my eye. Look now, for I shall not be here for your children to see.

"We hear you Dolphin, we hear you Rainforest . . . we hear you Mountain, Lichen, Condor. . . ."

One by one our stories pour out, filled with pain, with anger, and, occasionally, with humor. We all report how rapidly and radically humans are affecting our lives and our chances for survival. Yet the words carry, too, a sense of kindred spirit, for we are all of the same Earth.

When the flow of expression begins to subside, our ritual leader Frank, taking off his mask as Weeds, comes into the center of the circle. It is the first time in the ritual that we hear someone speak as a human.

We hear you, fellow beings. It has been painful to hear, but we thank you for your honesty. We see what we're

destroying, we're in trouble and we're scared. What we've
let loose upon the world has such momentum, we feel
overwhelmed. Don't leave us alone—we need your help,
and for your own survival too. Are there powers and
strengths you can share with us in this hard time?

No other signal or instruction is needed to shift the mood
of the Council. The grim reports and chastisements give
way to a spontaneous sharing of gifts.

As Slug, I go through life slowly, keeping close to the
ground. I offer you just that, humans. You go too far,
too fast for anyone's good. Know carefully and closely the
ground you travel on.

Water says,

I flow on and on. I deal with obstacles by persistence and
flexibility. Take those two gifts for your lives and your
work for the planet.

I, Condor, give you my keen, far-seeing eye. I see at a
great distance what is there and what is coming. Use that
power to look ahead beyond your day's busy-ness, to heed
what you see and plan.

Thank you, Slug . . . thank you. Water . . . Condor,"
murmur the humans.

One after another the beings offer their particular powers
to the humans in the center. After speaking, each leaves
its mask in the outer circle and joins the humans in the
center, to receive empowerment as a human from the other
life-forms.

As Lichen, I work with time, great stretches of time. I
know time is my friend. I give you that patience for the
long haul. I would relieve you of haste.

I, Rainforest, offer you my powers in creating balance
and harmony that enable many life-forms to live together.
Out of this balance and symbiosis new, diverse life can
spring. This I can offer to you.

As Dead Leaf, I would free you from your fear of death.
My dropping, crumbling, molding allows fresh growth.
Maybe if you were less afraid of death, you'd be readier

to live. I offer you companionship with death, as you
work with the natural, healing cycles of life.

Wildflower speaks.

I offer my fragrance and sweet face to call you back to
life's beauty. Take time to notice me and I'll let you fall
in love again with life. This is my gift.

I feel Mountain wanting to speak through me again.

Humans, I offer you my deep peace. Come to me at any
time to rest, to dream. Without dreams you may lose
your vision and your hope. Come, too, for my strength
and steadfastness, whenever you need them.

I take off my mask and join the group of fellow-humans
in the center. Hands reach out to pull me in close. I feel
how warm and welcoming is the touch of human skin. I
am beginning to gain a fresh recognition of our strengths.
For all the gifts that the beings offer are already within us
as potentialities, otherwise we would not have been able
to articulate them.

The last of the beings gives its blessings. Frank has
taken up his mask again and speaks:

I offer you our power as Weeds—that of tenacity.
However hard the ground, we don't give up! We know
how to keep at it, slowly at first, resting when needed,
keeping on—until suddenly—crack! and we're in the
sunlight again. We keep on growing wherever we are.
This is what we share with you—our persistence.

We thank him and pull him into our midst. A wordless
sounding arises. Grasping hands, we stand and begin to
move outward in a circle, laughing and humming. Sheila
leads the long line of us back in upon itself, coiling
gradually tighter and closer around ourselves into a group
embrace. It is the ancient form from this land's aboriginal
tradition known as a "humming bee." The close
intertwined embrace, cheeks against shoulders, skin on
skin, feels good, as the humming of our throats and chests
vibrates through us. It is as if we are one organism.

The hum turns to singing. Someone takes the drum. To its rhythm some move and dance, leaping and swaying and stamping the ground. Others move off among the trees and down to the waterside, to be quiet with themselves and what has happened.

Later, as the sun sets, we reassemble to release the life-forms that we have allowed to speak through us. A fire has been kindled in the growing darkness. One by one we come forward with our masks and put them in the flames, honoring the beings they symbolized and letting them burn. "Thank you, Condor." "Thank you, Mountain."

Tomorrow the circle will meet again, to speak of the changes we as humans will work for in our lives and in our world. Then we will make plans for action, hatch strategies, concoct ways of supporting each other. Right now it is good simply to rest upon our ground and watch the masks curl and crackle as they catch fire.

The Testimony of Graham Innes

Graham Innes

It's 5:24 AM as I pack away my sleeping bag and thin foam mat. This is the third day I will have spent buried up to my neck in clay and my right arm chained between two logs—they in turn being part of a fiddlesticks combination linking my hole with Graham Platts.

The first two days saw us buried against the bulldozers for eight and ten hours at a time while we refined our burial techniques to minimize pain and cramping. Also a slow dawning of awareness of a hitherto unknown connection. Earth bonding. Her pulse became mine, and the vessel, my body, became the vehicle for her expression.

I felt a strange serenity. There was no fear in the waiting, rather a calm understanding that this was right action that stood above the laws of the land, or rather, was in keeping with the highest laws of the land. This nonviolent action had been forced upon us as a last resort to save the Daintree Rainforest from the blades of men unhinged by greed, prestige and authority.

John Williams was the first arrestee, having leapt from an embankment onto the roof of the back-hoe cage where he chained himself to the machine's exhaust. A swift and daring action, but like most actions, shortlived. During the morning the back-hoe worked relentlessly, digging out those buried in holes and chained by their feet. One by one we were arrested.

Shortly after midday the police, working with bolt-cutters, moved to the last line of defense. Conservationists chained by their hands or feet to the front row of the huge fiddlesticks logs were removed one by one with the aid of bolt-cutters and chainsaws. But the use of the chainsaw was of little use as the logs had been heavily spiked to minimize or stop such action.

About 2 PM the last line of defence had all but crumbled, leaving Maria sitting cross-legged on top of a pole deeply embedded in the earth, chained by her foot—and the two Grahams buried in their holes beneath the pile of fiddlestick logs.

The back-hoe operator set to, to remove the logs when a cry went up as watching conservationists realized that our lives would be imperiled if an attempt was made to remove the logs in this fashion. The movement of a log at one end would set in train a movement of all the logs between which we were narrowly wedged. A halt was called while police sought to verify this information. Meanwhile the back-hoe operator had parked his vehicle in a position which allowed me direct eyeball contact. This was the opportunity I had been waiting for. Unknowingly preordained. The language was mine and I was speaking from the heart—and yet it was not of me. It was as though nature had overtaken my consciousness to speak on her behalf.

Directing my full attention to the back-hoe operator, almost forging a psychic link, my voice commanded attention:

Sir. You are stripping the earth of her mantle and she will die. She will die as surely as the naked baby left unclothed on the beach in the mid-day sun. Dying slowly but certainly of exposure. Stripped of her mantle and laid bare to the harsh unfiltered rays of the sun, the earth slowly sterilized. No longer allowing nature's vitality and fullness to work the miracle of creation.

Sir. I ask you to see that all of man's constructions surely fall into decay and within a brief period are to be seen no more. But nature, given her opportunity, continually recreates herself, providing a bounty, the fullness of which is beyond measure.

Sir. I ask you to desist from this act of madness, from taking part in this vandalism. Please withdraw. Go home now with honor. A hero whose praises of courage will be sung by all. There will be no shame, no stigma attached to such a decision. I know that in your heart you know it to be so. Act now and withdraw a hero. Listen to your heart. I see you hesitate. This is not the time for hesitation when your heart speaks to you of right action.

Sir. Sir. Can you hear me? I know you hear my words yet they seem to fall on deaf ears. Do words fail us then? Is this the silent testimony of the forest? If the words I use no longer touch your sensibilities, if they have become so trivialized as to become meaningless through overuse, then feel the energies of the forest. The pulse of life that surrounds you.

Sir. I do not believe that you cannot feel it. You must see before it is too late that it is the earth that sustains us, that continually recreates itself to sustain the diversity of species which live upon her surface. Sir. I call upon you in the name of humanity and on behalf of all of nature to take the right action. Go home sir. Go home. Do not allow words to fail humanity. To fail to convey her finest sensibilities in such an hour. Allow them to touch your heart and awaken the sensibility that I know must lie within. Go home a hero. Not in shame. Sir. I am not here as some joker. A fool for your amusement. I did not bury myself for that or to play some other game. I am here for the earth and the forest. Please understand my meaning. It is plain. You strip the earth of her mantle. The cloak which protects her and all of life. And you kill the earth. It is already plain to see. Go home sir. Go home . . .

Words fail. You rob her of her last vestiges and lay her to waste. Words have failed to provide the answers and now I see that they have failed to touch your sensibilities. I can only stand mute as the trees.

The hundred or so spectators and participants be they police, conservationists or council workers had long since fallen completely silent, and I spoke as though in an auditorium. Tension mounted. The back-hoe operator, anguished, his face contorted in agony as he sought to find the courage to withdraw, but could not. The police were obviously affected. They were immobilized, almost mesmerized by the words. The tension was too great—it was clear that they could no longer work and maintain the decorum demanded in a televised situation. The back-hoe operator backed off. The police withdrew for a two-hour lunch.

After the lunch break the assault by police and back-hoe operator began anew, only this time with a fierce determination that no words could crack. Like ants the police crawled around us, scooping out the earth tightly compacted around our bodies, and sheltered by the logs. A crane was brought in to remove a stump teetering dangerously above my head. The crane's jib was raised, and the crane and stump lurched drunkenly back from the site. Without room enough around me to work, the police were forced to dig under the logs in order to gain access for the bolt-cutters to free my chained arm. As the bolt-cutters clamped onto the already skin-tight chain encompassing my right wrist, it tensed so that it felt as though my wrist would be crushed in the process. I cried out for them to stop.

"Bullshit! He's putting it on," called two nearby police. Again they clamped the cutters. But this time a cop eye-balled me.

"Stop, you'll crush his wrist" he yelled. And the digging continued. At last they were able to manuever the bolt-cutters without causing the chain to twist and tension. Three hefty policemen, arms interlinking, operated the bolt-cutters. Snap. The chain was through. Now they were free to dig in front where my arm had been chained as an effective barrier. One by one, the logs were lifted clear to give access to the shovels. At last they had me.

Gatha for
All Threatened Beings

Ah Power that swirls us together
Grant us Bliss
Grant us the great release
And to all Beings
Vanishing, wounded
In trouble on earth
We pass on this love
May their numbers increase.

—Gary Snyder

Guidelines
for a Council of All Beings
Workshop
Joanna Macy and Pat Fleming

In response to the progressive destruction of the biosphere, Arne Naess called for a perspective and set of values he called "deep ecology." The name and the idea have caught hold around the world. Earlier in this book, Naess also calls for a form of community therapy or experiential process by which we can genuinely appropriate the perspective and values of deep ecology, and develop an ecological sense of the self. The group process called the "Council of All Beings" is intended to do precisely that. It is only one of the many forms which will undoubtedly arise to help us humans move beyond an anthropocentric and exploitative mindset in relation to our natural world, but it is a form that is already present among us and whose power is already known. A central aim of this little book is to share that form more widely.

The name "Council of All of Beings" has come to be used in two ways. In the narrower sense, it refers to a ritual form, a council circle of one-and-a-half to two or three hours, where people gather to speak on behalf of other species. The term is also used more inclusively to refer to a longer process, one that runs from one to several days and includes exercises and activities leading up to and flowing from the ritual proper. This process amounts to a workshop, often held over a weekend. In the workshop setting, the ritual council takes on more authenticity for the participants and seems effective in engendering change in their lives. We offer guidelines here for the more encompassing form.

There is nothing esoteric about conducting this form of group work. It is a natural and easy way to help people expand and express their awareness of the ecological trouble we are in, and to deepen their motivation to act. We do not need to be ecological experts or charismatic group leaders. The essential is already present in our desire that life go on, the desire which led us to pick up this book. Beyond that nothing more is required than clear intention, a place which is large and private enough for people to feel at ease, and a modicum of skills which can be acquired in guiding groups.

THE INTENTION

Starting with a clear intention as to our purpose in this work will carry us through difficulties or drudgeries it may present. Our efforts are made much easier by remembering that we do not need to "make it work" for our own sakes, but that we are simply, for the sake of all beings, offering a structure through which energy can spontaneously flow.

The primary aim of the Council and its workshop is perhaps just this: to enhance human commitment and resources for preserving life upon our planet home. This purpose happily includes a number of other subsidiary objectives:

—to foster compassion for all our fellow beings and to sharpen awareness of the dangers and difficulties they face
—to become more conscious of the commonality of our fate
—to motivate sustained action on behalf of all beings
—to remember and appropriate our larger lifestory through the long evolution of life upon this planet
—to take strength and authority from that larger, longer lifetime of ours
—to open ourselves to the resources of courage, endurance and creativity which are available to us in the web of life
—to become whole again, healing splits between mind and body, reason and intuition, human and nature
—to play together, giving permission and scope to our imagination and to the child within
—to build trust and a deeper sense of community with our fellow humans
—to prepare together for joint actions in defense of Earth and of future generations

What all these objectives amount to—and the list could go on, if we were to itemize all that people have experienced in the Council of All Beings—is a shift from the shrunken sense of self, to which our mainstream culture and its institutions have conditioned us, to a larger, more ancient and resilient sense of our true ecological Self.

PLACE, TIME AND NUMBERS

The Council of All Beings has been held in a wide variety of settings indoors and out, from the Grand Canyon to a college student lounge, from a grove of towering redwoods to a midwestern police armory, from a school gymnasium to a church sanctuary.

Numbers of participants have ranged from fewer than a dozen people to more than one hundred, and have included people of all ages.

The Council's duration has been as short as an hour-and-a-half and as long as four days. Choose what is feasible for the people you want to involve.

PREPARING TO LEAD A WORKSHOP

{Read Chapter Four of Despair and Personal Power in the Nuclear Age *(New Society Publishers, 1983) by Joanna Macy which details the requirements for leading a Despair and Empowerment workshop. They are essentially the same as for leading a deep ecology workshop, a Council of All Beings. Pay attention to the sections on leadership roles and styles, on varying the pace, on working with the breath and the body, on the uses of sound and silence, and on dealing with the release of intense emotions. Heed the importance of having worked with your own emotions. Leaders must have encountered the depths of their own inner responses to the dangers of annihilation of life and moved beyond their fear of these powerful feelings.}*

To guide a Council or a Council workshop, a delicate balance is required of the leaders. On the one hand, they offer and orchestrate a preconceived structure and need confidence in it in order to keep the process "on track." On the other hand, they must play the role of facilitator with enough humble ordinariness and flexibility to allow people to believe in the naturalness of the process and in expressing themselves genuinely and spontaneously.

Because as leaders we are inviting people to engage in an activity that is novel for them and risks appearing contrived or silly, it is all the more important for us to see these people in the perspective of deep ecology: that is, for us to address and believe in *their* larger ecological selves. No need to preach or push, only to allow people to open to the wisdom and pain that is hidden in each being as an intrinsic part of this beautiful and endangered world.

It helps to have training in group dynamics and experience in facilitating the expression of deeply felt concerns. It helps, equally, to have already participated in a Council of All Beings workshop. But these factors, while desirable, are not essential. The kind of skills you need to guide a Council can be developed.

Plan to share leadership of the Council workshop with one or two others, especially if you are new to it. Working with an experienced facilitator is the best training. Co-leading has two other advantages: it models for all involved the synergistic cooperation integral to the ecological perspective. And, as you alternate responsibilities for different parts of the workshop, each of you can participate more freely, expressing your own feelings and knowings more fully. Don't forget critical evaluation and mutual feedback afterwards, as important to effective co-leadership as careful preliminary planning.

Children enjoy participating in the Council of All Beings. At an early age they are able to understand its purpose and to derive encouragement and comfort from it. Less conditioned to feel separate from the natural world and to censor what they perceive, they have much to offer. An intergenerational Council has its own particular power and delight.

Children under the age of ten can become restless and distracting if expected to sit through the full process. They also can inhibit the older participants from expressing their fears, anger and sorrow about the condition of our world. If you decide to include them, arrange for childcare and decide which portions of the proceedings you will invite them to share.

THE WORKSHOP STRUCTURE

In the group work done to date, the reclamation of our ecological selves has involved three generic approaches. They consist of mourning, then remembering, then speaking from the perspective of other life-forms. Each approach or stage of the work can be served by a variety of exercises, some of which are detailed later in this chapter. Let us first see how these stages unfold within the chronology of a workshop, following upon the affirmation/clarification of intention and culminating in the making of plans for action and change.

GROUP INTENTION

We meet because our planet is in trouble. We meet because we who are party to the destruction of our biosphere must also be part of the healing which must occur.

As John Seed said at the start of a workshop:

> When a group of people gather together for a day or more with the intention to help each other heal our separation from nature, this shared intention is itself the healing we seek. So it is important to dwell upon this intention, to fix it firmly in our minds and hearts. Let us meditate for ten minutes now on this sacred intention.

If a workshop is longer than one day, people are urged to hold that intention very consciously as they go to bed the first evening.

The commitment to appreciate and serve life is made evident in the opening introductions. As people say their names, they are invited to speak of one (only one!) particular, ordinary aspect of the Earth that they love. If time allows, they can also tell what errand or felt urgency brings them to the Council. Sometimes we pass around an Earthball of ceramic or rubber or a stone or crystal for people to hold as they speak.

THE MOURNING

Deep ecology remains a concept without power to transform our awareness and behavior unless we allow ourselves to feel— which means feeling the pain within us over what is happening to our world. The workshop serves as a safe place where this pain can be acknowledged, plumbed, released. Often it arises as a deep sense of loss over what is slipping away—ancient forests and clean rivers, birdsong and breatheable air. *It is appropriate then to mourn—for once, at least—to speak our sorrow and, when appropriate, to say goodbye to what is disappearing from our lives.* As participants let this happen in the whole group or in small clusters, anger and fear and hopelessness arise, too— and something more, a passionate caring.

Caring, and the interconnectedness from which it springs, emerge as the ground of this anger and grief. It is an important part of the workshop leaders' role to point that out. Why else do we weep for other beings and for those not yet born? Deep ecology serves as explanatory principle both for the pain we experience on behalf of our planet and its beings and for the sense of belonging that arises when we stop repressing that pain and let it reconnect us with our world.

This stage is very similar in nature to the Despairwork, and it is preliminary to the other stages for several reasons. It erodes the culturally conditioned defenses of the separate ego, the fictions that "I" am or should be in control, that I can hold aloof from what befalls others. Secondly, mourning lends authority to notions of our interconnectedness or deep ecology. And, thirdly, it deepens trust between members of the group for all the work that follows.

The time allotted to this stage need not be long. What is essential is to help people tap into the authenticity of their caring and move beyond fear of the pain it entails. For that purpose one or several of the following exercises can be helpful.

Telling Our Eco-Stories

This exercise is for the opening session of the workshop, as it lets each person be heard at length from the outset. In groups of three of four, participants take a specific amount of time (five to fifteen minutes) to recount particular life experiences in which they felt powerfully the presence of the natural world and/or felt pain over what is befalling this world. The leaders can model this for the whole group, and then emphasize that this storytelling is not a conversation; people are to listen to each other attentively without comment. A bell or drum can mark the time allotted to each person, and let silence surround each one's story.

In introducing this exercise, Joanna often quotes the words of the poet Thich Nhat Hanh: *What we most need to do is to hear within ourselves the sounds of the Earth crying.* Each of us hears these sounds in a different way. How have you heard them?

Meditation Upon Chief Seattle

The eloquent and prophetic words of this great Native American chief over a century ago and recreated by Ted Perry in 1970 can serve as a "scripture reading" for deep ecology work. The text of his testimony is passed around the circle, each person reading a short paragraph aloud, in a strong voice, please. (See page 67 for Chief Seattle's testimony, divided up into suitably short paragraphs.)

At the close of the reading, the leaders let a silence occur, and then invite those present to speak what is in their hearts. "We can speak as if to Seattle himself, here in our midst, telling how it is now for us and for our fellow-beings." There will be no lack of response, for Seattle touches a deep chord. What follows is usually a cleansing "speak-out." Its role in the first half of the workshop is similar in function to the confession of sins near the start of the Christian liturgy; without it we risk hypocrisy in thinking of ourselves as agents of wholesome change.

Honoring Endangered Species

This is a ritual form similar in function to the Chief Seattle exercise. Several voices simply read aloud from the list of threatened and endangered species. (Available through organizations for the preservation of wildlife. The meditation "Bestiary," page 74, can also be used for this purpose.)

After each name of plant or animal life now facing extinction, a pair of sticks or clackers are struck sharply together, with finality, like the sound of a guillotine—for extinction is forever. Since we stage no funerals for other species as they pass from our midst, it is appropriate to hold them at least for a moment in our collective attention, honoring the particular qualities they brought for a while to this Earth we share.

Leave time at the end of the reading for spontaneous response from the whole group. The leaders can invite this response to come in as pure sound, beyond words. Tapes of whale song can elicit and embrace this sounding, which often takes the ancient form of keening, allowing tears which are appropriate and want to be shared.

The Eco-Milling

A nonverbal form of interaction that gets people moving around the room or space, this exercise is a kind of guided meditation through successive, silent encounters between people. As they move or mill about, upon spoken cues from the leader, they pause again and again in front of another person, taking their hand and beholding this being, this life-form in all its intricacy and vulnerability. Relieved of the necessity to respond, participants can direct full attention in accordance with the leader's suggestions—attention to the being they now see and touch, to the human form that has evolved over millions of years, that now feels grief for its world, that has powers within to act and rebuild.

This deeply evocative and powerful exercise is easy to lead.* Let the silent encounters which you invite people to make honor their concerns for life and the dangers they face in this time:

> As you look in the eyes of this being, let the possibility arise in your mind that this person may die of cancer from something they breathe or drink from our environment.
> . . . That possibility is part of being alive in this planet-time and you are strong enough to face it and deal with it . . . Without words acknowledge this in any way which feels appropriate.

In the same fashion, invite the people as they face each other in pairs to "let the possibility arise in your mind that this person before you may play a decisive role in the healing of our world. . . . " Let them respond spontaneously to that eventuality as well. The exercise can be expanded to include space for increased personal sharing:

> As you walk, notice how a human body feels. Now approach someone elses, someone you don't know and take their hand in yours. Taking turns of a couple of minutes each, tell them of a special time, of a strong

---

*Read the description of "The Milling" in *Despair and Personal Power in the Nuclear Age* (New Society Publishers, 1983), page 94. Then adapt it to the context, giving additional emphasis to the ecological crisis.

experience you have had within Nature, something that
stands out for you and remains with you . . . now thanking
each other, begin to move around around the room again
at your own pace, taking time to breathe fully as you
move . . .

Other exercises described in *Despair and Personal Power in the
Nuclear Age,* such as the guided meditation called "Breathing
Through" and the imaging exercises which use colors or clay,
are also suitable for this stage of deep ecology work. They both
allow, with the silent support of the group, repressed concerns
about our world and its future to come to the surface. As this
material is acknowledged and integrated in conscious
awareness, energy is released for creative response.

REMEMBERING

As organic expressions of life on earth, we have a long and
panoramic history. We are not yesterday's child, nor limited
to this one brief moment of our planet's story: our roots go
back to the beginning of time. We can learn to remember
them. The knowledge is in us. As in our mothers' wombs our
embryonic bodies recapitulated the evolution of cellular life on
earth, so can we now do it consciously, harnessing intellect and
the power of the imagination.

Certain methods help trigger this remembering. They are
various guided meditations focused on our evolutionary
journey, evoking our four-and-a-half billion-year story as Earth
(or our fifteen billion-year story as the universe.) Here are some
forms which have been used fairly extensively to good effect.

Evolutionary Remembering

The Evolutionary Remembering (page 45) can serve as the
cognitive basis from which you can build and lead the forms
you choose. It is offered here as a two-part exercise. The first
part takes us through the story of the universe from the "Big
Bang" to the beginnings of organic life on earth. It is best
offered as a narrative, a story. In preparation, ask group
participants to sit or lie in a comfortable position, where they
can remain alert and relaxed. The narrator reads slowly, with

pauses, as s/he invites a journey of remembering back to the very beginnings of the universe.

The second part is a guided movement meditation on the evolution of organic life from single cell existence through the complexities of form and expression possessed by present-day humans. We explore the steps of human evolution, replacing the primitive creation myths with the reality of our actual journey. (Participants act out this remembering, "feeling," as it were, the process of their own evolution.)

Allow one to one-and-a-half hours for this excerise. Begin by asking participants to lay on their backs or bellies, in a comfortable position, relaxed and breathing easily. In this guided meditation, ask them to begin each evolutionary stage by imagining fully, in their mind's eye, the movements being described before beginning to move. Some people will prefer to experience the whole exercise as a visualization, sitting quietly. Encourage the participants' authentic responses to the instructions, allowing them to move as much or as little as they wish. Participants are often surprised by how much their bodies already know. In the more mobile stages, participants may find physical contact with others an appropriate response, but they should be asked to beware of human conditioned responses, like apologizing. A drum or rattle may be used to signal the end of a stage, instructing participants to come to a resting position before the next set of instructions.

Allot a half-hour at the end to allow people, sitting or stretching out in pairs, to review the process verbally. Describing to each other how it felt in the mind-body to remember being *lizard* or *small mammal* makes it more vivid and assists the recall.

This meditation through sound and movement assists us in experiencing levels of awareness below that of words, giving us a powerful sense of the untapped memories and wisdom within the cells of our bodies.

Our Life as Gaia

A text for this is offered on page 57. It can be read aloud, or learned and extemporized with your own variations and additions, both to small groups and large audiences. Do it, if you can, to the sound of a drum, drumming a heartbeat, the heartbeat of each of us and the heartbeat of our world.

The Gaia Meditation

Presented here on page 41, this form is also well suited to large groups and congregations. It is especially effective, however, when people are seated in pairs facing each other. They serve then as each other's "meditation objects," as we evoke the wonders of our biological nature and the dynamic elemental flows which sustain and interweave our beings.

The Cradling*

If you lack time or space for the whole process—an hour and room to recline—a simple cradling of another's hand can be done to great effect. With large audiences, this five minute process can be inserted into a speech, program or religious service. In workshops it can be used in tandem, or as a substitute for the "Eco-milling" as one of the nonverbal encounters people are directed to make. Invite participants to close their eyes, so that all their attention can be directed to the sense of touch.

> Note the intricacy of the bone structure and musculature, the soft, sensitive padding of palm and fingertips. No shell or armor here, or protective padding. This is clearly an instrument for knowing as well as doing. Through it our earth can touch itself and know its shapes and texture . . .
> You could be anywhere in the universe, in any dark corridor of space, and if you encountered that object you'd know you were home. For it's a human hand of planet Earth. You don't find that anywhere else. It took four-and-a-half billion years and the particular conditions of this planet to make it . . . It was a fin once in the primordial seas where once we swam . . .

Let your words evoke its story, how it pushed up on dry land, learned to reach, to grasp, to fashion tools, to weave and plant,

---

*The text of The Cradling is given with instructions in *Despair and Personal Power in the Nuclear Age*, page 101, and can be adapted to emphasize the evolutionary aspect for the sake of our remembering.

to build temples and telescopes, gas chambers and hospitals.
. . . work which is in store for it in the times that are coming,
work in building a sane and decent world.

In working together to develop an ecological sense of self,
we rediscover how ancient we are. As a workshop leader you
can remind people of the authority and endurance with which
that great age endows us. When in defense of living species we
stand up and speak to corporations, government officials or the
military, we don't do it out of personal whim or passing fancy—
but with all the authority of our four-and-a-half billion years!

Eco-Breath

Another exercise for reintegrating the human into the biosphere
is called "Eco-Breath" designed by John Seed and Robert Rosen
in Australia. It is based on a workshop form called BRETH
(Breath Releasing Energy for Transformation and Healing), a
pathway of personal growth similar to "Rebirthing" where
connected, holotropic breathing is used to put oneself in touch
with deep, unconscious levels of our being and to come to terms
with unresolved situations in our past that limit and condition
our present life.

In a rebirthing group, people choose a partner and take turns
being "breather" and "sitter." In a session which typically will
last several hours, the breather lies down and by adopting a
particular breathing rhythm, may experience profound insights
into deep areas of their being. This may be accompanied by
intense visions and memories, strong feelings and emotions,
weeping, shaking, raging and so forth. A sense of problems
solved, healing, integration and empowerment typically follows
several rebirthing sessions.

BRETH is similar to rebirthing, but adds considerable
emphasis on the *intention* with which the person enters the
breathing session. The intention is consciously formulated, and
in the group sharing and discussion following the sessions, the
breather's experience in the session is usually found to relate
closely to his/her intention. In the Eco-Breath workshops, we
spend two days in BRETH sessions. In the second set of
workshops, the intentions change from personal, biographical

to planetary. These sessions have proven effective in reaching transpersonal, even trans-species levels of our being.

For more information about Eco-Breath workshops, contact John Seed c/o Rainforest Information Centre, PO Box 368, Lismore, New South Wales, Australia.

IDENTIFYING WITH ANOTHER LIFE-FORM

Through mourning and remembering, the workshop participants have opened to the universality of the life within them. They are ready to shake off their solely human identification and for a while imaginatively enter the experience of another life-form. It is as satisfying to do this as it is to resurrect a half-forgotten skill or after years to sing a once familiar song. The workshop helps us feel our way. We choose— or let ourselves be chosen by—another species. Harkening to the whispers of the natural world around us and within us, we stretch to see and feel what lies just barely beyond our human knowing.

We prepare, in other words, for the ritual of the Council of All Beings. And the preliminaries involve three stages: letting ourselves be chosen by another life-form, making a mask to represent it, and practice in speaking for it.

Being Chosen

In inviting people to let themselves be chosen by another life-form, you can speak much as Frank did in the narrative of The Council of All Beings earlier in this book. When working out-of-doors in nature, give at least an hour to this process, urging people to go off alone and find a place which feels right to them as on a Vision Quest—which this part of the workshop is often called. The participants are finding an ally to speak for in the Council.

If you are working indoors, the quest is entirely internal and the time can be as short as ten or fifteen minutes. Play an audio-tape of wilderness sounds or a meditative drone; avoid music which might distract or direct attention. Ask people to relax deeply, preferably lying down, and to wait with an open, non-discursive mind as they invite the presence of another life-form to join them.

Whether working indoors or out, encourage people to stay with the first impulse that arises. It is not a question of choosing a species you think you know a lot about, but rather allowing yourself to be surprised by the life-form that comes, be it plant, animal, or ecological feature, such as swamp or canyon. Ask people to visualize this being fully and from every angle, its size and shape and ways of moving. Ask them to request this being's permission to enter it, so they can imaginatively sense its body from within. Finally, let them ask the being how it wishes to be represented and what symbolic form can be made as a mask to be worn in the Council.

Mask-Making (in silence)

Lay out the materials (cardboard, color markers, paste, tape, scissors, string, etc.) on groundcloths or tables. Have people work without speaking. You can encourage relaxation, spontaneity and creativity by playing a tape of nature music. The originality which emerges in the concoction of these workshop masks is often remarkable.

The masks can either be attached to the head by string, elastic, or by taping the mask to a stick which can be held before the face. The latter is preferable for the purposes of the Council as it is more easily manueverable as participants shift from their human to their other life-form and back again. Be sure everyone cuts holes to see and speak through; a mask which blocks the mouth makes hearing that being difficult. Some people prefer to make a breast plate or to paint their face. Whatever the choice, emphasize simplicity and ease of movement with the mask on.

A half-hour should suffice. When the time or setting available to a Council does not allow for mask making, you can give people small squares of paper—or blank sticky labels—and let them simply take a moment or two to draw a shape or symbol of their life-form. When even that is not feasible, given the size of the gathering or other considerations, don't be overly concerned. Participants in the Council can simply announce who they are.

Moving Meditation on the Life-Form

If time allows, this exercise helps people identify more fully with their life-form. Masks are set aside.

> Sitting comfortably or lying on the ground, relaxing and breathing easily, begin to let yourself feel how it is to take body in this new life-form . . . What shape are you? . . . How much space do you take up now? . . . What is your skin or outer surface like? . . . How do you take notice of what is around you? move, if indeed you move at all . . . Do you make any sounds? Play with these sounds. . . .

Practice Speaking for the Life-Form

Donning their masks and in small groups of three or four, participants are given the opportunity to practice using their human voice to speak for their adopted life-form. This process, like the preceding one, deepens identification. Without such preliminary work, the beings in the Council risk speaking from too human a perspective—moralizing, blaming, or loading their utterances with generalities and scientific data.

Invite each being to speak in turn for five minutes to their small group, introducing themselves and expressing how it feels to be who they are. Urge them to stay focused on their physical nature and way of life, avoiding pronouncements on present environmental conditions.

> Gifted fully with the power of speech, tell how it feels to be you. What are the strengths and qualities you especially enjoy? Try to stay true to your new being and speak in the first person. And those listening can ask questions to assist the speaker to express and know its being more thoroughly.

The process often brings much laughter and mutual delight. It is so effective in demonstrating to people their capacity for identifying with other life-forms that it is sometimes used in lieu of the Council of All beings when there is insufficient time for the Council ritual to be held. In those cases, the content that the small groups address is expanded into three stages. After portraying the nature of their experience, the beings are invited to tell how life has changed for them under the present conditions that humans have created in the world. Lastly, they name the particular powers or gifts they would offer to humans to help them stop the destruction that is going on.

The Council of All Beings

The narrative in this book (beginning on page 79) can serve as a guide in leading the ritual proper. Remember that each Council, being essentially the extemporaneous expression of those present, is different from all others. Each has its own character and flow. Some release torrents of intense feelings, others appear lighthearted or relatively staid. Remember, too, that appearances can also be misleading: participants who seem awkward in their roles, or relatively silent and uninvolved, can be deeply affected by the Council.

While the opening of the ritual is preplanned, the nature of its ending can never be foreseen. How it concludes depends on the mood of the group and the dynamics unleashed. Some Councils wind up reflectively in silence. Some end intimately as the humans in the center hum or chant, or with reverence as each mask is placed on a wall or makeshift altar and thanks offered to the being it represented. Other Councils burst into hilarity with spontaneous drumming and dancing, with hoots and howls and other wild calls. Still others have ended with several of the above in succession.

At the closing of the ritual or soon after, the adopted life-forms are released, allowing people to withdraw from identification with them. Preferably this is done by a ritual burning of the masks, one by one around a fire. Each person thanks their Being as they put their mask into the flames, while the rest of the group joins in saying, "Thank you, owl," "Thank you, Sahara . . . "

Allow two hours for the ritual Council, and let the time following the day's work be relatively unstructured. It is good to rest and relax together after the evening meal, telling stories or giving messages, dancing or just watching the night sky.

THE FOLLOW-UP:
INTEGRATING AND PLANNING

When the group reconvenes in a large circle, begin by letting people share their personal reactions to the Council ritual. They need to express some of their reflections on the experience, and some of the inner responses it stirred in them, before they can concentrate well on anything else.

The first portion of the hour is not a discussion. Remind people of this as you invite them to speak at random, and leave a moment or two of silence between utterances so that they can hear each other better without need for comment. These expressions can take the form of song, movement, spoken words, and can include the dreams which came in the night. This time can deepen the experience the participants have had together, as well as their sense of community.

Now, after some minutes for moving and stretching, is the time for planning work together. How are we drawn now to act in the world? What changes do we want to make in our lifesytle? What actions do we feel inspired to undertake? How can we help each other in this work?

You can start with brainstorming ideas, with scribes noting them on sheets of newsprint. The ideas which arouse special interest can be discussed as a whole group or in small clusters. Now is the time to become concrete, to share information and resources—books, tapes, organizations. And now is the time to make specific plans for actions and subsequent meetings. Be sure that the next steps are determined before the workshop ends.

THE CLOSING

As is appropriate to the depth of the Council of All Beings workshop, its ending takes a ritual form. This can be as simple as a standing in a circle where thanks and reverence are expressed for the life which pulses through us all, and spontaneous prayers and commitments are uttered. It can be a more elaborate ritual designed and offered by the participants. The closure should include a thanking, honoring and releasing of the four directions, if these were invoked at the beginning.

The Council workshop is now over in one sense only. While it is unlikely that this particular circle of beings will meet in its entirety again, it will continue in the thoughts of all those present as a part of their internal landscape, reminding them of their larger, truer, ecological self.

Appendix: Sample Workshop Agendas

These are examples of workshop formats we have used for one- and two-day events. They reflect only a sampling of the wealth of exercises, meditations, and rituals we have used in the Council of All Beings over the past three years. Each format aims to include the essential features that lead participants to a fuller understanding of deep ecology, and their individual roles within it.

ONE-DAY FORMAT (9 AM – 5 PM)

9 AM	– Registration and orientation to workshop environment
9:15	– Physical warmups/breathing exercises/games/ chanting, etc.
9:30	– Welcome and introductory talk
9:45	– Introductory exercise
10:00	– Eco-milling
10:20	– Evolutionary remembering
11:30	– Time alone with Nature/finding an ally
12:30	– Lunch break and mask-making
1:45	– Voice/body warmups. Whole group check-in
2:00	– Meditation on chosen life form
2:15	– Small groups to interview each other as life-form
2:30	– The Council of All Beings Ritual opening of ritual space

readings
Bestiary/list of threatened species
introduction of beings present
invitation to humans to join as silent witnesses
further responses from beings to humans
humans ask for guidance
time alone in nature to bid farewell to being
ritual releasing of the being
closing of the council

4:00	– Pairs looking at how to live deep ecology values
4:15	– Brainstorm on what is "work for the planet?"
4:25	– Pairs focus on what our individual work and commitment is/will be and what support we will need over the next year
4:40	– Report back/closing circle—evaluation, remarks, "humming-bee"/song

(Note: This is a fairly intense schedule designed more for indoor work. If the workshop is outdoors, lengthen the schedule by at least an hour to match the slower outdoor pace.)

TWO-DAY WEEKEND WORKSHOP
(Friday, 7 PM to Sunday, 4 PM)

Friday, 7 – 9 PM

7:00	– Registration/orientation
7:15	– Welcome and introductory talk
7:30	– Introduction exercise
8:00	– Game/songs/choosing affinity groups
8:20	– Affinity groups meet—affirm individual intentions for the weekend
8:50	– Goodnight story/songs

Saturday, 9 AM – 9 PM

9 AM	– Warmups/stretches/game. Review of day
9:20	– Affinity groups meet and design opening ritual
9:50	– Opening of ritual space by affinity groups
10:10	– Eco-milling
10:40	– Evolutionary remembering
12:00	– Time alone with Nature; finding a special place for quiet thought
12:30	– Lunch break
2:00	– Whole group check-in/game
2:15	– Readings—Bestiary/list of threatened species— ending with Chief Seattle reading/exercise
3:00	– Vision Quest—finding our ally (time alone)
4:00	– Mask-making
4:30	– Exploration of new being—meditation, and in pairs
5:00	– Dinner break
7:00	– Our Life as Gaia meditation
7:20	– Affinity group meets—listening time on whatever is unfinished; then designing eco-drama
8:10	– Performance of eco-drama
8:40	– Cradling exercise
8:55	– Goodnight song

Sunday, 9 AM – 4 PM

9:00   –   Announcements/description of day/group
           check in
9:15   –   Voice and body warm-ups
9:30   –   The Council of All Beings ritual
11:00   –   Time alone in nature
11:30   –   Affinity groups meet to examine their experiences
12:00   –   Lunch break
2:00   –   Whole group check-in/songs/games
2:30   –   Integration exercises—In pairs: How do we integrate
           what we've learned into everyday life?
           Brainstorm: What is our work for the planet?
           Small groups: What is/will be our personal work for
           the planet and what support do we need in this over
           the next year?
3:40   –   Closing circle—closing of ritual space/support
           networks/group benedictions toward all beings/final
           comments/humming-bee

Suggested Readings

BOOKS

Bly, Robert. *News of the Universe*. San Francisco, CA: Sierra Club Books, 1977.

Cornell, Joseph Bharat. *Sharing Nature with Children*. Nevada City, CA: Ananda Publications, 1979.

Devall, Bill and Sessions, George. *Deep Ecology*. Layton, UT: Peregrine Smith, 1985.

Houston, Jean. *The Possible Human: A Course in Expanding Your Physical, Mental and Creative Abilities*. Los Angeles, CA: J. P. Tarcher, 1985.

Kaufman, Les and Ken Mallory. *The Last Extinction*. Cambridge, MA: MIT Press, 1986.

LaChapelle, Dolores. *Earth Wisdom*. Silverton, CO: Finn Hill Arts, 1984.

Massey, Marshall. *In Defense of the Peaceable Kingdom*. Santa Rosa, CA: Pacific Yearly Meeting Social Order Committee, 1984. (Order from Robert Schutz, 789 St. Helena Road, Santa Rosa, CA 95404 for $US 3.50.)

Myers, Norman. *Gaia, Atlas of Planet Management*. Garden City, NY: Anchor Press/Doubleday, 1984.

Macy, Joanna. *Despair and Personal Power in the Nuclear Age*. Philadelphia, PA: New Society Publishers, 1983.

Maddern, Eric. *The Human Story*. London, UK: The Commonwealth Institute, 1984.

Snyder, Gary. *Good Wild Sacred*. Madley, Hereford, UK: Five Seasons Press, 1984.

Snyder, Gary. *The Old Ways*. San Francisco, CA: City Lights Books, 1977.

Snyder, Gary. *Turtle Island*. New York, NY: New Directions, 1977.

Starhawk. *Dreaming the Dark: Magic, Sex, and Politics*. Boston, MA: Beacon Press, 1982.

Starhawk. *The Spiral Dance*. San Francisco, CA: Harper and Row, 1979.

Swimme, Brian. *The Universe is a Green Dragon*. Santa Fe, NM: Bear & Company, 1984.

RESOURCES

Rainforest Action Newsletter
300 Broadway, Suite 28, San Francisco, CA 94133
Monthly newsletter and action alerts.

Earth First!
PO Box 5871, Tucson, AZ 85703
Newspaper promoting environmental direct action and deep ecology
published eight times a year.

Creation
Friends of Creation Spirituality
Box 19216, Oakland, CA 94619
Quarterly magazine exploring all aspects of "creation spirituality"
and its social implications.

Raise the Stakes
Planet Drum Foundation
Box 31521, San Francisco, CA 94131
Journal of bioregional and ecodecentralist thought and politics.

ReVision: Journal of Consciousness and Change
66 Church Street, Cambridge, MA 02138
Quarterly.

New Catalyst
Box 99, Lillooet, British Columbia V0K 1V0 Canada
Probably the best journal of bioregional eco-philosopy in North
America.

VIDEO

Earth First
The video "**Earth First**" detailing the ongoing nonviolent struggle
to save the Daintree Rainforest in Tasmania, Australia, is available
on VHS for $39.95 (plus $7.00 shipping and handling). Order
from the Educational Film and Video Project, 1529 Josephine Street,
Berkeley, CA 94703, (415) 849-1649.

About the Authors

John Seed is director of the Rainforest Information Centre, New South Wales, Australia. Since 1979, he has been involved in the protection of rainforests in Australia and throughout the world. He is editor of the World Rainforest Report and has assisted in the formation of rainforest action groups in the United States, Japan, and Europe as well as in Third World countries where most of the rainforests are found. In 1986, he co-produced with Jeni Kendell the film "Earth First," an hour-long documentary history of the struggle to save the Australian rainforests. He travels extensively around the world lecturing on the plight of the rainforests and conducting Councils of All Beings and other "re-Earthing" workshops.

Joanna Macy is a teacher of world religions, and an activist in movements for peace and justice. She is the author of *Despair and Personal Power in the Nuclear Age* (New Society Publishers, 1983) and *Dharma and Development* (Kumarian Press, 1983), a book about the Sarvodaya self-help movement in Sri Lanka. Thousands of people have participated in her workshops in North America, Europe, Asia, and Australia. Joanna is co-founder of the international Interhelp Network, a global network of people from all walks of life who strive to integrate political, emotional, and spiritual dimensions of the work for peace and justice.

Pat Fleming is currently living in Devon, England where she is involved in setting up an Earth-Care college. Over the past ten years she has worked with and led a wide range of workshops and courses, five years as a psychologist and social worker exploring alternatives to traditional psychiatry, and five years working with peace, evironmental and women's groups in Great Britain, Australia, New Zealand and the United States. She helped establish and develop the Interhelp Network in Great Britain and Australia. For the past several years she has concentrated on conducting Council of All Beings workshops and other empowerment tools using voice and movement.

Arne Naess is Professor Emeritus of Philosophy at Oslo University in Norway. In 1973, he coined the term "deep ecology." He is a renowned Spinoza scholar, and has written extensively on Spinoza, Buddhism and Gandhi. He has also engaged in nonviolent acts of ecological resistance. Dolores LaChapelle, in *Earth Wisdom* tells of an incident in which Naess, an accomplished rock climber and Himalayan mountaineer, tied himself high on the wall of a Norwegian fjord and refused to descend until authorities dropped plans to dam the fjord. The authorities backed down and Naess roped down.

Dailan Pugh (illustrator) is a prominent artist living in the rainforests of northern New South Wales, Australia. He has participated in direct actions to protect the forests and has worked on their behalf for a decade. He has written and illustrated a series of childrens' activities books on Australian habitats, several natural history texts, as well as a guide to the rainforests of northern New South Wales. He is currently working for the New South Wales National Parks and Wildlife Service in the educational program division.

The authors of this book are conducting Council of All Beings and other "re-Earthing" workshops in the United States, Europe and Australia. For information regarding these workshops, write:

Pat Fleming, Caroline Wyndham
30 West Street
Ashburton, Devon UK
Tele: (0364) 52932

Justin Kenrick
The Salisbury Centre
2 Salisbury Road
Edinburgh EH 16 UK
Tele: 667-5438/9802

Interhelp US
PO Box 8895
Madison, WI 53708 USA
Tele: (413) 586-6311

Joanna Macy
1306 Bay View Place
Berkeley, CA 94708 USA

John Seed
Rainforest Information Centre
PO Box 368
Lismore, New South Wales
2480 Australia
Tele: 066-218505

Publisher's Note

I am writing this note the day of the birth of my daughter Aliyah Shanti which literally means "peace arising."

Like virtually all expectant parents, we had been looking forward to her birth. The birth of children, whether biologically ours or not, allows us to "borrow from eternity," for children provide us a glimpse of a future which, at least within the boundaries of our limited physical selves, we can never know.

But we also approached Ali's birth with fears which would have been unknown to our ancestors, but which are now widely shared. We worried, mostly silently and in our nightmares, about environmentally-caused birth defects. We worried about whether we could find a place to live that was free enough from industrial or agricultural pollution or urban ruin to be "fit for children." As we waited for Ali to arrive, it seemed our eyes grew keener at spotting the destruction around us. Two weeks before Ali's birth, when my partner Ellen and I went into a supermarket to buy paper diapers (just for travelling; we insist on using cloth at home!), Ellen burst into tears at looking at shelves and shelves of what must once have been forests. I do not worry about whether we can provide for Ali's college education; I *do* worry whether I am doing enough to prevent nuclear war so that she will get that far.

Twice today, I have turned on the television and unintentionally found myself rooted to tales of the near-extinction of the black-banded ferret in the hills of Wyoming and of the African elephant on the Serengeti plain. Twice on this day I have opened the newspaper to read about the evacuation of sea otters from the Monterey coast to a new "preserve" which (it is said) will prevent the species from extinction in case of oil spills (six of the twenty-four died in the process), and then of the unexplained poisoning of thirty-eight rare brown pelicans only miles from my home.

When I allow myself the emotional space to reflect upon these phenomena, I realize again and again that it is really only one phenonemon: the impending death of the planet caused by our own "life-support" systems. We are witnessses, held in thrall to, and are even perversely fascinated by our executioner—our own death-dealing modern industrial civilization, fueled in part by our own greed and preying upon the fact that we have lost any true sense of who we really are.

We can, we *must* regain that sense, or discover it anew. Without it, we have already died a death more horrible than any we can imagine. That process of rediscovery will not be easy and will not come without struggle; virtually all the forces of our culture, our society, our daily life and what we pass off as an educational system are arrayed against it.

What John Seed and his colleagues bring to this struggle comes naturally to Ali: a sense of new wonderment at our interconnectedness, a way of looking at the world through primordial eyes. In a culture whose god is a narrowly-defined efficiency, it is a sensibility which we associate with poets and dreamers, a way of seeing thought to be both inaccessible and perhaps even inappropriate to our daily lives. The special contribution of John Seed, Joanna Macy, Pat Fleming and Arne Naess is the certain knowledge that this insight, this way of seeing—no, this way of being—is not a function of individual creativity nor something which we can afford to shun, but is our common birthright, one which we renounce, consciously or unconsciously, only to our deepest peril.

It is in the spirit of the recovery of this birthright, one I already can see in my daughter's eyes, that New Society Publishers is proud to publish *Thinking Like a Mountain: Towards a Council of All Beings*.

David H. Albert
for New Society Publishers
Santa Cruz, California
24 October 1987